© Copyright: 2018 Andreas Krennmair

First Edition, February 2018

Text: Andreas Krennmair

Cover Image: Brotzeit des Klosterschäfflers by Eduard Grützner, 1912

Cover Design: Andreas Krennmair

Publisher: Andreas Krennmair, Erasmusstr. 1, 10553 Berlin, Germany

ISBN: 9781980468523

All rights reserved. Except for use in a review, no portion of this book may be reproduced in any form without written permission of the publisher. Although the author and publisher have made every effort to ensure that the information in this book was correct, the author and publisher do not assume and hereby disclaim any liability to any party for any loss, damage, or disruption caused by errors or omissions, whether such errors or omissions result from negligence, accident, or any other cause.

Contents

1 Foreword   1

2 Introduction   5

3 Historic Ingredients   9

    3.1 Malt 10

    3.2 Hops 11

    3.3 Yeast 14

    3.4 Water 16

4 About The Recipes   19

5 Historic German Beer   21

6 Bavarian Beer   25

    6.1 Bavarian Weissbier 32

    6.2 Munich Lagerbier 40

6.3	Munich Winterbier	46
6.4	Bamberger Lagerbier	48
6.5	Augsburger Lagerbier	54
6.6	Salvatorbier	57
6.7	Oktoberfest-Märzenbier	60

7 German White Beers — 63

7.1	Berliner Weisse	65
7.2	Broyhan	73
7.3	Gose	76
7.4	Kottbusser Bier	80
7.5	Grätzer/Grodziskie	84

8 German Brown Beers — 91

8.1	Berliner Braunbier	93
8.2	Fredersdorfer Bier	97
8.3	Mannheimer Braunbier	99
8.4	Braunschweiger Mumme	102
8.5	Merseburger Bier	105

9 Historic Austrian Beer — 109

9.1	Horner Bier	111
9.2	Carinthian Stone Beer	113

9.3	Vienna Lager	118
9.4	Prague Beer	121

10 Converting Historic Recipes 123
    10.1 Units 124
    10.2 Converting a Recipe by Example 126

11 Acknowledgments and Dedications 129

12 Glossary 131

13 Bibliography 135

Chapter 1

Foreword

The German-speaking region of Europe has a wonderfully diverse and rich brewing heritage, extending back over a thousand years, that (along with that of Great Britain) can undeniably be considered one of the two great pillars of influence in brewing today.

The industrialisation of brewing and the many wars on the European continent in the 19th and 20th centuries led to a disconnection from this brewing past. The passage of time and commercial interests further separated today's beer drinkers with the many varieties of beer that were consumed for hundreds of years.

However, as new interest in beer grows around the globe, commercial brewers and homebrewers alike are looking for authentic links to the past. Britain's brewing heritage has been explored in detail and has been the main influence on the successful craft beer movement of the last forty years, while the brewing heritage of the German-speaking world has been largely ignored.

There are several reasons for this:

1) The first craft beer brewers of the US started brewing top-fermented beers in the British tradition (pale ales, IPAs, porters & stouts) in direct contrast to the less flavourful, mass-produced lager that had saturated the market.

2) It is much easier, time- and cost-efficient to brew top-fermented beers than bottom-fermented beers. This is especially true for the home-brewers, who would later go on to found many of the most successful craft beer breweries operating today.

Largely for these reasons, the brewing heritage of the German-speaking region is still largely unknown, even if it is generally revered in hushed tones! When efforts have been made to dig out an old beer style, history is often obscured by myths and short cuts that do not accurately represent how such beers were brewed centuries ago.

I met Andreas through the small, but quickly growing homebrewing community in Berlin several years ago. Humble, enthusiastic, analytical and with a good eye for detail, Andreas was always interested in historical recipes. Through his own brewing experiments, I was able to sample beer styles that I would not otherwise have had access to.

I was delighted when Andreas told me about this project. It was through Andreas that I first learned about Broyhan, Fredersdorfer Bier and Mannheimer Braunbier. It is high time for a detailed collection of historic recipes based on authentic, referenced sources (in the German language).

The project that Andreas has undertaken here is a gargantuan task. Hopefully, it will find an audience of like-minded brewers, who will also be able to provide feedback on both the recipes and any historic documents they may have access to. This being a first edition, I have no doubt that there will be additions and revisions in future versions, but I know that Andreas will incorporate any improvements enthusiastically, as it brings us all closer to our brewing heritage.

Although the false myth of the so-called 'Reinheitsgebot' still captures the public imagination, it is time for home-brewers to discover and reintroduce new audiences to the authentic brewing heritage of the German-speaking region. This book goes a long way in enabling this.

Prost!

Rory Lawton

Berlin, May 2017

Chapter 2

Introduction

My first contact with beer was at a very young age, even before I went to school. Beer wasn't exactly a daily staple at our household, but my father would sometimes have a beer on the weekends with lunch or dinner. My brother and I would often be allowed a sip of foam when we asked. There was a certain fascination about it, as it was a grown-up drink, but in the end it didn't really taste nice, way too bitter for the palate of a five year old boy.

My proper beer drinking began for me at the age of 16, the legal drinking age in Austria for beer and wine. Beer in Austria in the late 1990's was relatively dull. People ordered "a beer", which meant a medium-hopped golden lager of whatever was the house brand. If you wanted to be different or just have something different, you'd order Hefeweizen, Bavarian cloudy wheat beer, and if you wanted to be particularly sophisticated, you'd go to an Irish-themed pub and drink Guinness. Friends of mine thought Heineken and American Bud (which at that time was sold as simply "Anheuser Busch" due to the ongoing name disputes with Budweiser Budvar) were great, exotic beers. I usually had whatever was available.

When I moved to Berlin in early 2009, the beer there was not much different compared to Austria: standard lagers, some of them even duller than the Austrian stuff, some more interesting and more highly hopped and drier, others a lot maltier. Berliner Weisse, the local beer style associated with the city, was more of an oddity. Work colleagues who have lived in Berlin since the early 1980's told me to basically ignore it because the only commercially brewed Berliner Weisse available at that time was nothing like Weisse from 30 years ago.

In summer 2011, I visited a school friend in New York City. While he was an avid proponent of Austrian lager beer, I had my first contact with a beer which at that had been mythical to me: India Pale Ale. Around 2010/2011, it was the first time that I had read about this beer style, but even though I looked, I couldn't find any such beer in Berlin. So New York was the first time I actually had the opportunity to try beer like that. And it was certainly a revelation. The way the hops resonated in these beers was completely different from anything I had ever tasted before. My palate was completely untrained, and so while I couldn't pick out any particular aromas or flavours, I vividly remember that the hopping not only added this intense layer of completely new tastes, it even seemed to change the overall mouthfeel of it: it was almost like a tickling on the tongue. With the exception of one particular beer, the now-retired Sam Adams IPA, I can't even remember which ones I had, but it certainly got me interested. And I can proudly claim that I didn't have a single American macro lager while I was in New York!

Upon my return, I started looking a bit into local breweries, and I found a microbrewery that had their brewing kit and a bar in my local district's market hall. They actually had an IPA, but it was just not quite as vivid and impressive as what I had in the US.

In late 2011, I met my now wife. She's from the United Kingdom, and so the first time we went to London together, she introduced me to another beer thing that I had never tried before: cask ale.

And it was another revelation: low-alcohol beers, packed full of flavour, and most pubs we went to had a large variety of them. People didn't just order "a beer" in the US or the UK, they ordered specific beers of a large selection, and some of them would even specifically seek out the good stuff.

We eventually started exploring the then-emerging craft beer scene in Berlin, and at some point, we also started brewing our own beer. In fact, we got very much into homebrewing, and brewed all the beer types that we wanted to drink but couldn't really get in Berlin. And from there it was a deep dive down the rabbit hole: I started reading about brewing. A lot. Mitch Steele's book "IPA" was my first touchpoint with historic beer. Ron Pattinson's blog "Shut up about Barclay Perkins" was fun to read, as well, and gave me some great insights into how beer used to be. Those were really the starting points that motivated me to look into historic brewing by myself. It started with just downloading a few historic English brewing books that I found online, and reading and trying to understand them.

From there, I then went on to German brewing books. And suddenly I realised how much there was around about historic German brewing: the beer styles, the beer culture around them, it was so completely different from how we know German beer today. It just got me excited, there was this huge treasure of historic beer, of German history, that seemed mostly forgotten. I easily managed to get hold of a lot of historic books that described some of these beers with enough details that I was actually able to rebrew them at home. That was living history for me.

Initially, I didn't put much structure into what I was reading and writing down, but at some point, I realised that I just had to do my research in a more structured way, write down all the little bits and pieces about brewing in general, and analyse and present historic brewing recipes in such a way that they'd be useful for homebrewers. That's where the idea of writing a book came from. This book is my attempt to make this piece of German history available to homebrewers, to make old beer styles that had simply fallen out of fashion 150 to 200 years ago more accessible to interested people, and to show what a rich and diverse beer culture Germany used to have that was essentially replaced with quite uniform, industrially produced lager beer, with only a few local strongholds that had partially resisted this take-over.

Simply due to the availability and accessibility of historic sources, I put my focus on beers of the late eighteenth century and nineteenth century. At that point in time, brewing technology was so advanced that German brewers were already working with thermometers and partially with hydrometers, which allowed a great reproducibility of documented brews, while at the same time, old, traditional, local beers were still in production and hadn't been supplanted by fashionable Pilsner-style or Bavarian-style lager beers yet. Because of that, this time period gives a great insight into a bygone era of brewing, but with a precision that makes it possible to reconstruct these old beers.

Chapter 3

Historic Ingredients

The beer recipes in this book were put together based on historic sources. If available, specific recipes and processes were described, but for some beer styles, only very general information about ingredients, colour and general flavour was passed on. This makes it particularly hard for brewers to achieve the same flavours, aromas and overall consistency as the historic originals.

3.1 Malt

In most historic beer recipes, the aspect of how the malt was produced is unclear, and how historic descriptions, like brown malt and amber malt, correspond with modern malts. Since the first half of the 19th century was a time when a lot of brewing technology was modernised, and e.g. Bavarian breweries started introducing more modern, "English-style" smoke-free kilns, while other breweries still operated smoke kilns, it is quite unclear which malts were smoky, which ones were not, and if they were smoky, to what extent. Recipes in this book will so say in their ingredient lists if they specifically require smoked malt.

In order to facilitate the reproduction of these beers with available ingredients, I decided to only include modern malts. I therefore used Munich malt in recipes that called for brown malt, Vienna malt as amber malt, while for pale and air-dried malts I assumed that they were most likely similar in colour to modern Pilsner malt. Essentially, the colour of the wort produced from the modern malt is equal to the colour description of the historic malt.

The way historic brown and amber malt were used clearly indicate that they must have had enough diastatic power to convert themselves. It would therefore be unwise to use modern brown malt in place of historic brown malt, or modern amber malt in place of historic amber malt, as modern malts of that kind do not have sufficient diastatic power.

Besides that, even when there exist some descriptions how historic brown malt was made, the vast majority of homebrewers don't have the equipment or the skills to reliably steep, germinate and kiln their own malt.

In the end, relying upon just modern malts makes the recreation of historic beers more accessible for most homebrewers. Especially for German beer styles, it will still be reasonably close to the original.

3.2 Hops

The earliest records of hop cultivation in Germany date back to the 9th century[14, p.2]. It is thought that the Hallertau, one of the main growing areas of hops in Germany, was the cradle of hop culture, from which it spread further north towards the river Danube, and later on further towards Franconia, in particular the Spalt region[14, p.3]. The first definite source that documents the conserving power of hops in beer was eleventh century Hildegard of Bingen, who wrote about the big significance of hop additions for preserving beer in her book "Physica"[14, p.5].

In the 13th and 14th century, hop gardens outside of Bavaria started to pop up: in Silesia, Brandenburg, Mecklenburg and Thuringia, hops started to get grown, while in Northern German cities like Lübeck, Hildesheim and Kiel, hop gardens were documented. Along the Rhine, hop beers were as popular as grut beers: some burghers of Dortmund asked the Holy Roman Emperor, Louis IV, for a confirmation of their brewing rights of grut beer, which was granted in 1332[14, p.8].

It was not until the 18th century though that German hop growing got another boost: in 1743, the Prussian king Frederick the Great complained about a lack of sufficient hop agriculture in Prussia and the subsequent necessity to import foreign hops, which led to a lot of money leaving Prussia. An important principle of economic policies at that time was self-sufficiency. Pomerania was therefore ordered to plant hop gardens, while Saxony had to grow enough hops to be at least self-sufficient, and if possible, to even export hops to neighbouring countries[14, p.9]. In 1751, he ordered that experiments with Bohemian hop seedlings shall be undertaken in the regions of Altmark and Kurmark, as Bohemian hops were more popular and more highly priced on the hop markets due to "their greater strength and power".

The Seven Years' War (1756-1763) took away the king's focus on hop growing, but in 1770 new initiatives were started to further promote growing hops for sulf-sufficiency. Hop poles were sold to farmers for a cheap price, and even a contest was started, with a cash prize for the farmer with the greatest hop production by the end of the year.

In 1775, more hop gardens were introduced in Western Prussia, and the king's chamber director was ordered to expand hop gardens around Potsdam since the existing ones weren't yet able to cover the demands in hops for brewing in Berlin. In 1776, hop imports into Prussia were completely prohibited due to a substantional surplus production.

After a bad hop harvest in 1777, the king didn't decide to allow imports, but instead, also forbade hop exports. This export ban caused the hop prices in Prussia to crash, making growing hops very unattractive for farmers, many of which abandoned that crop within the next few years.

Only when a terrible crop failure hit most European hop growing regions in 1860, Prussian hop agriculture briefly grew again: Hallertau was the only region with a good harvest, and therefore could sell their hops up to 6.5 times their normal price. This caused an increased interest in hops as an attractive cash crop. But by the end of the 19th century, much of Prussian hop growing had shifted to Posen/Poznań, while both acreage and yield in the rest of Prussia steadily decreased[14, pp.11-12].

In Württemberg, hops have been cultivated for a long time along its border to Bavaria, but because of the strong local wine industry, brewing wasn't nearly as important there. Only in the 19th century, more focus was put on hops as a cash crop, and hop farmers even received a tax relief in 1819 to promote hop growing. The hop industry in Baden and Alsace-Lorraine is about as young as the one in Württemberg, but developed into a hop growing region with a well-received export product during the

19th century. Württemberg was particularly successful with its crops from Rottenburg and Tettnang, while Alsacian hops were popular in Belgium and France[14, pp.13-15].

In the Austrian empire and later the Austrian-Hungarian empire, Bohemia was by far the greatest hop producer, with regions such as Saaz/Žatec and Glattau/Klatovy being major exporters, followed by Galicia, Styria (parts of which now belongs to modern Slovenia), and rather minor producers like Upper Austria, Carinthia and Moravia.

Until the middle of the 20th century, hop bitterness, in particular alpha acid content of hops, were not really well-researched. Hops in historic recipes are usually only provided in terms of weight or volume, only very rarely a particular type of hops is specified. Most often, just whatever hops were locally cultivated were used for brewing. Because of that, it can be assumed that a large amount of the hops that were used for brewing before the 20th century were local land races with a relatively low alpha acid content.

The recipes in this book therefore often don't specify any particular variety, but often suggest a sensible default, e.g. for most German beers, a German land race variety. A specific amount of alpha acid is assumed, which is provided with the recipe. If you want to brew a recipe, you need to adapt the amount of hops based on the alpha acid content of the hops that you'll be using.

Nevertheless, the suggested hop varieties were chosen based on locality: while Hallertauer Mittelfrüh is assumed as a "default" German hop, some recipes contain hops that are geographically more appropriate, for example Bohemian (Saazer) hops for Austrian and Bohemian beers. Some recipes for Bavarian beer styles also specifically prescribe the use of Saazer or Spalter hops.

3.3 Yeast

Until the discovery by Louis Pasteur in 1876 that yeast is a single-cell organism, the nature of yeast was not well understood. Through experimentation, brewers knew that it was somehow necessary for properly fermenting beer, and that certain treatment, such as too much heat, could damage it in such a way that it was unable to conduct any further fermentation.

Pure yeast strains were first grown from single yeast cells by Emil Christian Hansen at Carlsberg brewery in 1883. Until then, most yeast that was pitched most likely contained several yeast strains, and may have been contaminated to a certain extent with other bacteria. Bottom-fermenting yeast strains had the advantage that the low temperatures inhibited the growth of bacteria, which historically was the prerequisite to brew relatively clean and stable beers[64, p.16].

From historic records we know that some yeast strains, in particular bottom-fermenting lager yeast strains, had a relatively poor attenuation, which means that they were not able to completely ferment all fermentable sugar in the wort. While the attenuation of modern lager yeast usually range between 70 and 80%, lager yeasts up to the early 20th century only managed a much lower attenuation of 55 to 65%, quite often even lower than that. In fact, the legal limit of Bavarian beer was 48% attenuation, which posed a problem for brewers, as some of them produced beer with an attenuation lower than that. In practice, this law and its 48% limit were not strictly enforced, as the practical limit was considered to be 44%. In 1891, Colosseum brewery in Munich was found to be in violation of this limit, as their beer only had an attenuation of 41.86% even after 3 months of fermentation and maturation. Only after a court-appointed expert was able to determine that even lager beer from the state-run Hofbräuhaus brewery had an attenuation below 44%, all charges were dropped and the court proceedings were suspended[38, p.25].

For homebrewers nowadays, these numbers pose the opposite problem: modern yeasts have been selected to attenuate relatively highly, which makes it hard to find a lager yeast that is suitable for brewing historic beers. Of all the commercial lager yeast strains that are available to homebrewers, the strains available from White Labs known as WLP820 and WLP920 show a relatively low attenuation, and are therefore preferable for historically more accurate brewing.

Top-fermenting yeasts are even harder to categorise: while some historic brewing records suggest only a low attenuation for some beers, others on the other hand show a relatively high attenuation that was certainly higher than bottom-fermenting strains at that time. All of this does not even take different mash regimes into account that could produce worts with either very high or very low amounts of unfermentable sugars.

I can therefore recommend a relatively neutral top-fermenting yeast, such as White Labs WLP029, for top-fermented recipes. If you prefer dry yeast for homebrewing, other types such as Fermentis S-04, S-33, or Danstar Windsor Ale yeast work equally fine.

For Bavarian white beers, a yeast strain like Wyeast 3068 or White Labs WLP300 is suitable. For added authenticity, homebrewers can attempt to get fresh bottles of Schneider Weisse wheat beer, and build a starter out of its sediment. The authenticity for that yeast strain comes from its provenance: Schneider Weisse can directly trace the source of its yeast to the state-run Bavarian white beer breweries of the 19th centuryy[62].

3.4 Water

Water chemistry was not particularly well understood during the period covered in this book, but even just from practical experience, brewers knew that different types of water were more or less suitable for different beers. A distinction between hard and soft water was made, and brewers generally preferred soft water.

Three different sources of water were used: first, rain and snow water, as it was the softest since it did not come in contact with soil or rock where it could have dissolved salts[33, pp.71-72], but also the least reliable to obtain.

Second, river and spring water. The problem with river water was accessibility, though, as breweries needed to be reasonably close to a river. The use of rivers to dispose of waste was also problematic as it limited the times when river water could actually be drawn. Spring water was usually cleaner, but depending on the ground with which it had contact, it could vary a lot in composition[33, p.69].

Third, well water. This source was considered to be the worst, as it was often described to be foul, and always required boiling to clear up[66, p.16]. Depending into which soil the well had been dug, it was still more or less acceptable: gravelly or sandy soil was considered to be the cleanest, clay soil was less clean. Chalky soil was even worse due to the high chalk content that it caused in the water[33, p.69].

To treat hard water to make it suitable for brewing, several methods were employed. The easiest way was to simply boil the water to precipitate dissolved chalk. This was very resource intense since it required lots of fire wood. Another method was to let the sun shine on the water, and to aerate it using bellows or by pouring it over layers of straw or wood shavings[33, p.74].

This treatment only precipitated chalk, but not dissolved gypsum. To get rid of the gypsum, the water was treated with potash or cream of tartar. The use of activated charcoal (made from animal bones) between layers of sand as filter was also known to improve the quality of hard water[33, p.75].

For brewing historic recipes, I recommend to simply use unchlorinated tap water. Optionally, if you know that your tap water is particularly hard, you can boil it beforehand to precipitate calcium carbonate. Otherwise, just use whatever water that you would normally use in homebrewing.

Chapter 4

About The Recipes

If you intend to brew one of the beers described in this book, please be aware of a few words of advice that should make it easier for you to brew the recipe on your personal brewing system.

First, it is expected that you have previous homebrewing experience and are comfortable with brewing recipes according to a specified original gravity, grist composition, and hop schedule, and are able to follow more complex processes that very likely deviate from your normal practices. Providing an introduction into homebrewing is beyond the scope of this book, and other literature exists that can teach the fundamentals of brewing at home in a more understandable and concise way.

The recipes in this book will provide you with with an expected original gravity (provided in Plato and gravity points), an expected IBU (calculated according to Tinseth), an expected colour (provided in both EBC and SRM), and an expected ABV content that is based on the estimated attenuation of the final beer. In addition, the grist composition is provided both by weight and percentage. The weight is specified both in metric units (i.e. grams, kilograms, and litres) and US customary units (i.e. pounds, ounces, and gallons). Unless otherwise specified, all recipes are scaled to the same size. For *metric units*, it is expected to result in *20 litres of beer*, while for *US customary units*, it is expected to result in *5 gallons of beer*.

All malts used in this book should be easily available for homebrewers in homebrewing shops, as should all hop varieties. If you're unable to get a specific hop variety, please refer to the previous section about historic ingredients to find suitable substitutes.

As for the equipment, some recipes expect you to be able to do a multi-step mash with several rests at different temperatures, while others may require you to have a separate vessel in which you can boil parts of the mash. Please read the recipe and in particular the described process steps carefully to understand how the process works and what equipment you will need. When handling hot mash, liquor, wort, or equipment, please wear safety equipment to protect yourself accordingly from any injuries that could arise.

Chapter 5

Historic German Beer

Beer has got a long tradition in Germany. Already in the eighth century, beer was brewed in Bavaria, and later brewing spread to other parts of the Holy Roman Empire. The common ingredients back then were more diverse than nowadays: beer was often seasoned with herbs. Gruit (or grut) was the name for various proprietary herb mixes that were used for seasoning beer and whose ingredients entirely depended on the producer. Only later, hops became prevalent for their bittering and preservative qualities.

In Bavaria, the production of beer was regulated by various laws, most famously in 1516, nowadays dubbed the *Reinheitsgebot*, or "purity law". These laws were in effect only for a relatively short amount of time, and so brewing outside of the "purity law" must have been relatively common. The term "purity law" itself is a recent invention, its first documented use is from a session protocol of the Bavarian Parliament on March 4, 1918[19].

Outside of Bavaria, much more diverse and complex brewing traditions emerged, in which a large number of different ingredients were used. Be it juniper, marjoram, thyme, plums, fir rind, burnet, elderflowers, rose hips, honey, ginger, gentian roots, bitter oranges, lemons, oregano or cardamom, as long as the ingredient was not poisonous and added good flavours to the beer, both brewers and beer consumers were fine with them.

Despite this large diversity, German beer styles can still be categorised into two major groups of beers: Braunbier (brown beer) and Weißbier (white beer). Although nowadays Weißbier is synonymous with wheat beers, the original meaning only referred to the colour of the malt. Brown beers were brewed from kilned malts, which means that the germinated grains were dried over fire, which often resulted in a rather dark and smoky malt. White beers on the other hand were made from air-dried malt. This type of malt was not kilned, but instead just dried with a cool, unheated air draft. This production method was a lot more work-intense and time-consuming since the drying process was a lot slower, and the resulting malt couldn't be stored for long due to its still relatively high moisture content.

Some historic literature also refers to Gelbbier (yellow beer) and Rotbier (red beer), but since these were most likely also made from (lightly) kilned malt, they can be considered to be forms of brown beer.

When it comes to grain varieties used for malting, German brewing tradition was more diverse than it is nowadays. Besides the ubiquitous barley, there were also wheat and oat, and less commonly spelt, that found their use in malting. Wheat was a relatively expensive ingredient, while oats were generally perceived as cheap, and were most likely used as a low-cost filler material.

As for hops, most of the time hops were grown and used locally. Hops from certain growing regions were considered to be of higher quality than others. Hops were traded by origin: Bohemian (Saazer) hops were considered to be of the highest quality, and were thus the most expensive ones. Spalter hops had a similarly good reputation, even though a distinction between Stadthopfen ("city hops") and Landhopfen ("country-side hops") was made. Other important hops were Hallertauer, Aischgründer, Württemberger, Hersbrucker Gebirgshopfen ("mountain hops"), Wolnzacher and Auer hops, Upper Austrian, Alsacian, and Altmärker hops. These hops were often also divided into three quality grades, "prima", "secunda" and "tertia", which were priced differently[12].

Most beers used to be rather perishable and would sour easily, so they were only consumed locally. Only certain specialties, often beers that were brewed rather strong in original gravity and/or alcohol, highly hopped, or otherwise fortified against spoilage, became successful export articles that in some cases were shipped to other European countries or even halfway around the globe. But most beers just remained local, and already in the 19th century, the term "Lokalbiere" (local beers) was used to describe beers that were typical just for small regions, cities or towns. Most of them had rather colourful names, and unfortunately, that's often also the only information that we have about them nowadays. Low-alcohol beers were also often brewed by producing a "Nachbier" by rinsing the mostly spent grains yet another time, boiling this low-gravity wort with spent hops, and fermenting it like a normal beer. This drink was sold for very little money as refreshment, or sometimes used to dillute stronger beers. Common names for beer like that was often "Covent", "Kovent", or "Kofent", while in Bamberg, the local equivalent was called "Heinzele" or "Hainslein".

With the rise of exportable lager beers in Bavaria, Vienna, and Bohemia that could be sent all over Germany and beyond, the popularity of local beer styles diminished, and most of them disappeared, while others became local niche beers. Brewing made the shift from craft to science, and with the invention of refrigerators by Carl von Linde and the introduction of pure yeast cultures grown from single cells by Emil Christian Hansen, bottom-fermented beers became more prevalent all over Germany. Top-fermented beer styles only survived locally (e.g. Düsseldorfer

Altbier, Bavarian Weißbier, Berliner Weisse, Gose) or as imitations of pale lager beers (e.g. Kölsch).

Chapter 6

Bavarian Beer

For about 500 years, the vast majority of Bavarian beers, unlike most other beers in Europe at that time, were brewed in a bottom-fermented fashion, at cool temperatures, to give the beer time to slowly ferment and mature. These beers were fermented in cellars that were mined deep into rock, and sometimes filled with snow or ice to keep them cool during the warmer seasons. Most other beers were consumed quickly after the end of fermentation, with very little or even no time for maturation. Bavarian beers were different, they were stored and matured for several months, and were thus named after the German word for storage or warehouse, "Lager", so "Lagerbier" just means "beer that has been stored".

In the 19th century, Bavarian lager beer was known as a specialty and was shipped all around Germany and beyond. The Bavarian brewing methods and the bottom-fermenting yeast spread over Germany and to neighbouring countries. Vienna lager, Bohemian lager, and Bavarian lager beer, their associated production methods and the industrialisation that came with them revolutionised beer on a world-wide scale. Nowadays, the vast majority of beers consumed globally are pale lager beers.

The beginnings in Bavaria were more humble, though: in the 16th century, brewing in Munich was not at a high standard, so to cover the needs of beer in the Duke's court, beer from Einbeck near Hanover was imported. Duke Maximilian I. considered this beer to be so good that he even hired a brewmaster from Einbeck to brew this beer at the Hofbräuhaus, the state-run brewery in Munich. It is thought that this beer eventually developed into one of Munich's beer specialties, the Bock or Bockbier[61, p.21].

Traditionally, Bockbier was served to the general public as seasonal specialty only starting on the 1st of May, but in the beginning of the 20th century, it was poured by most Munich breweries all year round, except Hofbräuhaus, which would only sell it at the beginning of May for a week, and a small amount on Corpus Christi. Interestingly, Bockbier was considered to be a breakfast drink, and wasn't generally served in the evening[40, p.361].

As late as the 19th century, Munich lager beer was very different from modern beer. Lager beers were brown beers, made from kilned barley malt. Only through the introduction of modern English kilning methods it was possible for brewers to produce pale kilned malts without a smoke flavour. These techniques were explored in Vienna, and Pilsen/Plzeň in Bohemia, and resulted in Vienna lager, an amber lager beer, and Pilsner Urquell, the prototypical pale, golden lager beer.

Bottom fermentation was very likely a mixed fermentation of different yeast strains until the invention and popularisation of pure cultures by Emil Christian Hansen. These lager yeast strains, as historic sources show, had a rather poor attenuation, which certainly had a great impact on the overall impression of the beer: not only were these beers higher in original gravity than today, they also contained less alcohol, and had a much greater amount of residual sweetness. Attenuation of 19th century lager beers were often in the range of 50 to 55%, sometimes going up as far as 65%. Since the fermentation and maturation was cold, the risk of infection and the beer getting sour was a lot lower than with top-fermented beers at the time, and thus also made sure that the beer would keep better for export.

In terms of malt, hops and yeast, the various local Bavarian lager beers were quite similar. The major difference though was in the production process. Breweries in Munich, Regensburg, Augsburg, Bamberg, Kulmbach or Nuremberg each established different mashing regimes and hopping methods, each of which made a unique impact on the local beer. In most cases, decoction mashing was involved, while infusion mashing was more prevalent at some places.

For making barley malt, two-row barley was generally used[7, p.426]. Other barley varieties were known as well, such as four-row barley, which is described as having smaller grains, giving a lower extract and being cheaper than two-row barley but also less liked by brewers; and six-row barley, also known as winter barley, or "Turkish" barley, which is described as being more commonly used for brewing in England and France rather than Germany[58, pp.47-49].

In 1818, the first Munich brewery introduced an English-style kiln that would work with heated air instead of smoke, and by the mid-19th century it was reported that most breweries had stopped using smoke kilns altogether as very dark, smoky beers had mostly fallen out of fashion[7, p.409]. Mash tuns were still made from wood, while the brewing kettles to boil the decoction were generally made from copper. The heating of the copper kettles, or "coppers" as they are called, was often designed in such a way that it would not only heat the kettles themselves, but also heat up the air for the kiln[26, p.79].

In cases where smoke kilns were still in use, great care had to be taken which wood to use. Any kind of wood that would produce a lot of smoke was unusable, such as spruce, fir, or pine. Dried beechwood, birchwood, or alder were better suitable, but had to be free from any bark[26, p.80].

Top-fermented beers were more of a niche in Bavaria. There is strong evidence that for some time Schenkbier was top-fermented in Bamberg, but the only widespread top-fermented beer style in Bavaria was Weißbier. It was brewed from air-dried malt, sometimes also with a share of wheat malt, which also made it an oddity and a special case in relation to the various Bavarian beer laws since the middle ages.

Bavarian Beer Legislation

In order to control what ingredients are being used to brew beer, local Bavarian rulers undertook several attempts during the middle ages and early modern period to establish various laws that defined permissible ingredients that ordinary brewers were allowed to use. In particular the types of grain that served as starch source and the herbs to bitter and preserve the beer were heavily regulated: some of these laws only allowed barley in malted or unmalted form, while for bittering, only hops could be used. There are several hypotheses as to why nothing but hops was allowed: one is that other ingredients often had unwanted effects on the user, while another theorises that this could have been a power struggle against the producers of grut (gruit), proprietary herb mixes that were prevalent in flavour beer during the middle ages.

The regulation on the grain type sometimes served to keep the markets for bread production, beer production, and animal feed separate, and in particular to ensure a sufficient supply with wheat and rye for bread. A common saying used to be "wheat for cake, oats for the horses, barley for the beer". Nevertheless, special privileges were granted that allowed a few brewery owners to produce Weißbier using wheat malt. In Augsburg, a crop failure in 1433 led to a decree that ordered brewers to use oats as the only grain in their beer, which was repealed only in 1450. Also due to crop failure, it was not allowed to brew beer in Munich from

1293 to 1294 so that grain would first and foremost be used for baking bread[7, p.406]. In 1480, a decree was enacted in Munich that allowed brewing of white beer only using imported, foreign wheat[55, p.11].

In the discourse about German beer legislation since 1918, these old laws that regulated beer ingredients were called *Reinheitsgebote*, "purity laws". The most well known "purity law" is the Bavarian purity law of 1516. It is nowadays referred to as *the* Bavarian purity law, and is also claimed to form the basis for modern German beer legislation, despite fundamental difference.

Before 1516, several other laws were established: in Regensburg 1469, beer ingredients were limited to barley malt, hops and water. In Munich 1487, only barley, hops and water could be used. The purity law of Landshut from 1493 limited the allowed ingredients to malt (not specifying any particular grain), hops and water. In the same year, Bad Reichenhall allowed malt, hops and water, but the council would grant applications for using other herbs and spices in beer brewing if they were not harmful to people but rather wholesome. The use of yeast was implied at that time, and was certainly added as a fermentation aid, but was apparently not considered to be an ingredient that was worth mentioning. It was most likely also implied that grains needed to be malted before they could be used for brewing, but the malting was not a strict requirement that was explicitly mentioned in some of the law texts.

While the 1516 purity law harmonised and unified several previous laws, it wasn't in effect for very long: in 1551, a ducal decree permitted the use of coriander and bay leaves in beer. In 1616, duke Maximilian I. renewed the purity law and prohibited certain herbs and seeds, but explicitly allowed the use of salt, juniper and caraway seeds[54].

Since the 16th century until well into the 19th century, lager beer in Bavaria could only be brewed from Michaelmas (29 September) to Saint George's Day (23 April)[61, p.16][7, p.449]. The time from autumn to spring was therefore brewing time, while the rest of the year was to mature and eventually consume the beer. Depending on what season the beer was brewed for, it was called either "Sommerbier" (summer beer) or "Winterbier" (winter beer).

Sommerbier was matured for longer, as it was first brewed end of September and first consumed end of April, and is synonymous with Lagerbier. Winterbier on the other hand was brewed for the same winter season, and matured for only a few weeks before it was served. When a beer was described as "Schenkbier" or "Schankbier", it meant a beer that was brewed weaker, served quickly and not matured for long, and was usually synonymous with Winterbier.

Besides these, there were also double beers like Munich Bock and Salvatorbier that were brewed to be stronger, but were only allowed to be produced by specially licensed breweries, and could only be sold at certain times of the year.

In 1811, a law, the "Bierregulativ", defined exact amounts of malt that brewers needed to use in order to brew different types of beer: using 30 Metzen (1 Metze = 37.0596 litres) of conditioned malt, a brewer had to produce either 30 Eimer (1 Bavarian Biereimer = 68.52 litres) of Sommerbier, or 33 Eimer of Winterbier. This conflicted with some local brewing methods, such as the Bamberg approach of employing infusion mashing and producing both a regular-strength beer and a Nachbier (a small beer made from the mostly spent malt) called "Heinzele". Brewers would have had to switch to decoction mashing, and in order to do so, they also would have had to upgrade their coppers as their conical coppers were not suitable for boiling decoctions. The Bierregulativ was therefore criticised by the brewers in Bamberg at that time[35, p.94].

In 1861, the purity law in its modern form was first added to the law code of Bavaria, by prohibiting the use of anything other than barley malt and hops in the production of brown beer. Both regulations from 1811 and 1861 didn't so much have the health aspect in mind (the adulteration of food and drink using any kind of harmful substance had already generally been punishable by law), but primarily had tax reasons: it guaranteed the use of specific amounts of barley malt, which could then get taxed appropriately[54]. The use of malt and the prohibition of malt surrogates was strictly enforced, and offenders were put on trial. This surrogate prohibition went so far that even brewing journals and publications that accepted advertisements for surrogates of malt and hops got prosecuted, the only exception being the Allgemeine Hopfen-Zeitung from Nuremberg, as it had international circulation[7, p.407].

This strictness was criticised by some, in particular the brewery owners association of Vienna, who claimed that this strict prohibition was a hindrance to any progress in brewing, and even some contemporary beer writers who otherwise supported the "purity" of Bavarian beer saw adjuncts like maize or rice not so much as cheap malt surrogates, but instead as legitimate alternatives to regular malt due to their high starch content combined with a much lower protein content[7, p.407].

6.1 Bavarian Weissbier

One of the distinctly Bavarian beer styles that is still around nowadays is Weißbier, or Weissbier, as it's sometimes spelled, which literally translates to "white beer" in English. Modern Weissbier is a top-fermented beer with about 11 to 13 °P (1.044 to 1.052) original gravity. Nowadays, the beer is brewed with at least 50% wheat malt, it only has minimal hop bitterness, and has a distinctly estery and/or phenolic aroma and flavour that is usually compared to banana and cloves. Until a few decades ago, its popularity was strictly limited to Bavaria, and even there, it was seen more as a beer for elderly women than anything else.

Because of its high content of wheat, it is often assumed that the name actually refers to the wheat, not the colour white. "Weiß" (white) and "Weizen" (wheat) do indeed have a common etymological origin. But when looking at historic sources, it is quite clear that wheat malt didn't use to be an essential ingredient of Weißbier.

The origins of Weißbier apparently lie with Bohemian white beer that became popular in Bavaria in the late middle ages. With the various beer purity laws enacted in 1469, 1487, 1493 and 1516 in Bavaria or parts of it, brewing with wheat was prohibited for the common folk. Brewing Weißbier from wheat was instead an exclusive privilege that was first handed to the Degenberg dynasty, and was later taken back by the Wittelsbach dynasty, the rulers of Bavaria, when the Degenbergers died out. Producing Weißbier from wheat practically became a state privilege[54].

Only in 1798, this exclusivity was repealed, and privileges were sold to other breweries. State-run breweries were eventually sold or leased out. One of the leaseholders of one these breweries, in particular Weißes Hofbräuhaus in Munich, was Georg Schneider. In 1873, Georg Schneider started his own brewery, as the lease for Weißes Hofbräuhaus was about to run out. Since he was leaseholder, he had the brewing privilege and the right to all ingredients, and thus was able to take both the privilege and the original yeast from Weißes Hofbräuhaus over to his new brewery. That new brewery is now known as Schneider Weisse, but the brewery has moved their headquarters and production facilities away from Munich since then. So Schneider Weisse, in terms of their origins as business, as well as in terms of the originality of their yeast, have a well-documented provenance.

But what was Weißbier like back then? Historic sources show quite a few differences to the modern product. Today, Weißbier (white beer) and Weizenbier (wheat beer) are considered to be synonyms. Nowadays, if you wanted to name a beer in Germany after a grain, the beer needs to contain at least 50% of it in the total grist. But in the past, Weißbier had a different meaning.

Generally, beer used to be classified into Braunbier (brown beer) and Weißbier (white beer). The distinction was in the malt: kilning technology was very primitive, and well into the 19th century, smoke kilns were still in use. These smoke kilns not only gave all the malt a smoky taste, it was also rather hard to control the temperature with which the green malt was kilned. Under such circumstances, it was basically impossible to gain an exact control over the malt colour, so all kilned malt was brown and smoky. To produce a pale malt, the easiest option was to simply air-dry it. The green malt was spread out in a well-covered place with a constant draft to slowly dry it out without applying any additional heat. Of course, that process took a lot longer and was more laborious that kilning, and the resulting malt couldn't be kept for long because it tended to spoil quickly and get mouldy. With the difference in these malts, brown beers were made from brown (i.e. kilned) malt, while white beers were brewed using pale, air-dried malt.

When we look at historic sources, we indeed find an indication that Bavarian Weißbier was not necessarily brewed with wheat. The first indication is a book called "Die Bayerische Bierbrauerei oder die Brauerei der braunen Biere und des weißen Gerstenbieres, [...]"[37], written by Friedrich Meyer and published in 1830. The title translates to "The Bavarian beer brewery or the brewing of brown beers and of white barley beer, [...]" and just gives it away: white beer brewed with barley. In the book itself, the author writes that Weißbier is brewed from only slightly kilned malt or alternatively air-dried malt. There was a difference in fermentation as well: while brown beers in Bavaria were bottom-fermented, white beers were usually top-fermented, though occasional deviations are documented. Because of the top-fermentation, it could also be done in warm weather, and thus was a perfect beer to be produced during the summer[37, p.155].

The author also notes that if wheat is not too expensive, some wheat malt can be added, at a ratio of half a Metze of wheat malt for every Schäffel of barley malt[37, p.155]. A Metze is 37.06 litres, while a Bavarian Schäffel was 222.36 litres, so that means only about 14% of wheat malt in the overall grist. That's not a whole lot, and even totally optional according to the author.

Interestingly, the author also mentions that Weißbier in Bavaria is in decline, and he partially blames the brewers for it. Some of them even openly mentioned to him that "one had to deliberately make a bad Weißbier so that the brown beer can be sold more easily"[37, p.159]. He counters that top-fermented beers can be consumed 3 to 4 days after fermentation is completed and that they can be sold within only a few weeks which means less tied-up capital and less risk for the brewer.

The same author published an updated version of his book in 1847 under title "Die bayerische Bierbrauerei in all ihren Theilen [...]"[36]. It also contains a chapter about Weißbier. In there, the author makes a specific distinction between "weißes Weitzenbier" and "weißes Gerstenbier", i.e. white wheat beer and white barley beer, both of which were commonly called Weißbier. He again mentions that it's a beer style in decline, praises it for its refreshing qualities in the summer time, but also describes it as a drink that was more common in the countryside, and, because of its relatively low price compared to lager beer, popular among poor people.

The recipe described in 1847 differs from the previous one from 1830: this time, it's at least one Metze of wheat malt for every Schäffel of barley malt. But even that means only about 28% of wheat malt, although it can be more. Another difference of Weißbier compared to brown beer was the malt itself: the rootlets of malt for Weißbier was allowed to grow longer, which might be an indication that malt for Weißbier was more modified than lager malt[36, p.135].

Weißbier brewed from wheat on the other hand is described as made purely from wheat malt alone. It's described as less perishable than Weißbier made from barley malt. Other than that, the processes of brewing it are the same.

Other sources confirm the descriptions found in both of Meyer's book: in "Handbuch für Bierbrauer"[39] by P. Müller (published in 1854), the author describes Weißbier as top-fermented, with a grist of 1/2 to 3/4 Metzen of wheat malt per Scheffel of barley malt (a different spelling of Schäffel), and that it's brewed both in summer and winter. The author also provides information about the original gravity: 10 to 10.5% extract[39, p.259]. That's actually a bit less than modern Weißbier.

Pfauth[46] describes two versions of Weissbier: one version is brewed from equal parts barley malt and wheat malt, had an original gravity of about 12% and was brewed at the Hofbräuhaus in Munich. We can assume that this was the typical composition for Weissbier that was brewed in breweries with the privilege to brew with wheat. Another version mentioned in the same book is described as brewed from barley malt only and significantly weaker: about twice as much Weissbier is produced from a specific amount of barley malt compared to brown beer. It was only brewed in the summer and mainly consumed by the rural population.

In the early 20th century, Bavarian Weißbier started getting produced in a more modern fashion: they were brewed in the same strength as lager beer of that time, a greater hopping rate was used, and fully fermented beer was mixed with unboiled wort (first runnings) to produce a highly carbonated beer through bottle-conditioning. Furthermore, clear versions of Weißbier, probably the predecessor of modern Kristallweizen, were produced by fining Weißbier with isinglass[64, p.161].

Recipe 1 (1854)

- OG 10.5 °P (1.042)
- 4.4% ABV
- 10 IBU
- 5.5 EBC (2.8 SRM)

Ingredients

- 3.6 kg (7.5 lb) Pilsner Malt (93.5%)
- 0.25 kg (0.52 lb) Pale Wheat Malt (6.5%)
- 25 g (0.83 oz) Bavarian hops, e.g. Hallertauer Mittelfrüh (3% alpha acid)
- 1 pack of Bavarian Weißbier yeast, e.g. Wyeast 3068

Mashing

- Dough in malt with 6.4 litres (1.6 gal) of cold liquor in a mash tun with false bottom, rest 2 hours

- Bring 9 litres (2.25 gal) of liquor to a boil
- Drain most of the wort from the cold mash
- Slowly mix in boiling liquor under constant stirring until the mash has reached 53 °C (127.4 °F), then rest 45 minutes
- Mix remaining hot liquor with cold first wort and set it aside to cool
- Drain most of the wort from the mash and slowly bring it to a boil
- Skim all the scum that's forming while heating up
- When the wort starts boiling, slowly mix in parts of it back into the mash until it has reached a temperature of 62 to 65 °C (143.6 to 149 °F).
- Then add about half of the mash back to the wort, and boil it for 45 to 60 minutes
- Slowly mix in boiled mash back into the main mash while constantly stirring, until mash has reached a temperature of 75 °C (167 °F), then rest 60 minutes
- Move wort that you set aside earlier to the copper, add all hops
- Lauter, sparge main mash with 78 °C (172.4 °F) hot liquor and add to the copper until about 26 litres (6.5 gal) of wort have been collected

Wort Boil

- Boil wort for 60 minutes
- Add all hops at the beginning of the boil

Fermentation

- Chill wort to 20 °C (68 °F)
- Pitch yeast

Recipe 2 (1870)

This recipe is based on a description of the ingredients and the process of how Weissbier was brewed in the Hofbräuhaus in Munich[46, p.188].

- OG 11.8 °P (1.047)
- 5% ABV
- 7 IBU
- 5.8 EBC (2.9 SRM)

Ingredients

- 1.9 kg (3.95 lb) Pilsner Malt (50%)
- 1.9 kg (3.95 lb) Pale Wheat Malt (50%)
- 20 g (0.66 oz) Bavarian hops, e.g. Hallertauer Mittelfrüh (3% alpha acid)
- 1 pack of Bavarian Weißbier yeast, e.g. Wyeast 3068

Mashing

- Dough in malt with 12 litres (3 gal) of liquor at 33 °C (91.4 °F) temperature, stir for 5 minutes

- Draw a thick decoction (about one third of the mash), bring it to a boil, and boil for 30 minutes
- Slowly mix back decoction into mash to bring it up to a temperature of 45 °C (113 °F), stir for 2 minutes
- Draw a thick decoction (about one third of the mash), bring it to a boil, and boil for 45 minutes
- Slowly mix back decoction into mash to bring it up to a temperature of 58 °C (136.4 °F), stir for 2 minutes
- Draw a thin decoction (about one third of the mash), bring it to a boil, and boil for 15 minutes
- Slowly mix back decoction into mash to bring it up to a temperature of 70 °C (158 °F), stir for 5 minutes
- Rest for 1 hour
- Lauter, sparge mash with 78 °C (172.4 °F) hot liquor until about 26 litres have been collected

Wort Boil

- Boil wort for 60 minutes
- Add all hops at the beginning of the boil

Fermentation

- Chill wort to 17 °C (63 °F)
- Pitch yeast

6.2 Munich Lagerbier

Munich Lagerbier is the archetypal Munich beer. It is a dark lager beer of medium strength, malty, but balanced with its hop bitterness. Nowadays better known as Munich Dunkel, it was Munich's most favourite common beer style well until the 1930's.

In the 19th century, this beer was more highly hopped compared to modern examples of the style, comparable to a modern German Pils, but due to extended lagering of sometimes up to 8 or 10 months, this hop bitterness aged out and got a lot smoother and less noticeable than a modern highly hopped beer of comparable bitterness.

Beers in Munich were usually fermented at temperatures between 10 and 15 °C, while the yeast was pitched at temperatures of around 8 °C, sometimes even close to 0 °C. There were three different techniques for pitching yeast: pitching "dry" was one, "herführen" another one, where wort was mixed with yeast until a small fermentation has started, and then this yeast was pitched to the whole wort[15, p.15], and then there the "drauflassen" method.

Pitching "dry" didn't literally mean the use of dry yeast, but it instead meant that yeast was just pitched, without getting it into an active state of fermentation beforehand[36, p.175]. The method of "herführen" was described as requiring less yeast, effecting a more uniform fermentation, and producing better beer, so presumably the "herführen" acted as what homebrewers would call a yeast starter nowadays.

The third method, called "drauflassen", was a bit more intricate, as it required two separate worts for the same type of beer produced two days in a row: the first wort was pitched with yeast, and within a day, went into a state where fermentation had just begun. The next day, the second wort was added to the freshly fermenting beer. Even though this method required more coordination in the brewing schedule, it allowed for a healthy fermentation and required less yeast[46, p.133].

As for the hops, Bavarian land race varieties such as Spalter, Hersbrucker and Hallertauer Mittelfrüh seem suitable. Bohemian hops such as Saazer are suitable, as well, as the import of hops from Saaz/Žatec and Glattau/Klatovy for the use in Munich breweries is well-documented[55, p.15].

One author in 1863 even recommends using different hopping rates and blends of varieties depending on how long the beer was lagered and when it was served. Since the cellar temperature would rise over the course of the summer, beers that were lagered for longer and at slightly warmer temperatures towards the end, the hopping rate would need to be adjusted. When brewing beer from 12 Scheffel of malt, he recommends 24 Pfund of Kindinger or Wollnzacher hops for beer served in May or June. For the time from July to August, 34 Pfund of a blend of 50% Saazer and 50% Kindinger or Wollnzacher hops are recommended, while September to October, an even higher rate of 42 Pfund of Saazer or Spalter hops is proposed[65, pp.58-59]. For the recipes presented here, this would mean about 60 grams of hops for May and June, 83 grams of hops for July and August, and 103 grams of hops for September and October.

In order to ensure a consistent quality of all the beer within the cellar, the different batches were blended: when a batch was finishing with its primary fermentation, it was filled into lagering casks. By splitting up every batch evenly between all lagering casks, it was made sure that all of the beer was of the same quality and strength[33, p.299]. This was even done in a rather intricate manner: if ten casks were to be filled, then one tenth of the beer was filled into every cask, starting from the first. When more beer was filled into the casks, it was again evenly divided up between the ten casks, but this time, the filling would start from the second cask. In the third round of filling, it would start from the third cask, and so on. The reason for that was that most of the yeast flocculated and settled out after primary fermentation, and when transferring the beer into the lagering casks, a small amount of it would inevitably be carried along by the stream of beer. By changing the cask from which to start filling, this small amount of yeast was evenly spread among all lagering casks[58, p.119].

Recipe 1 (1834)

- OG 16 °P (1.065)
- 5.3% ABV
- 44 IBU
- 20.5 EBC (10.4 SRM)

Ingredients

- 5.25 kg (10.96 lb) Munich Malt (100%)
- 120 g (4 oz) Bavarian hops, e.g. Hallertauer Mittelfrüh (3% alpha acid); alternatively Saaz hops
- 1 pack bottom-fermenting yeast, e.g. WLP820 or WLP920

Mashing

- Dough in with 18 litres (4.5 gal) of liquor of about 10 °C (50 °F), 4 hours rest
- Slowly mix in about 9 litres (2.25 gal) of boiling liquor, until a mash temperature of 40 °C (104 °F) is reached
- Draw 9 litres (2.25 gal) of thick mash, slowly bring to a boil (over the course of an hour), then boil for one hour

Historic German and Austrian Beers for the Home Brewer   43

- Mix back thick mash while stirring, until mash has reached temperature of 55 °C (131 °F)
- Draw 9 litres (2.25 gal) of thick mash, bring to a boil, then boil for 30 minutes
- Mix back thick mash while stirring, until mash has reached temperature of 67 °C (152.6 °F)
- Draw 9 litres (2.25 gal) of thin mash, bring to a boil, then boil for 15 minutes
- Mix back thin mash while stirring, until mash has reached temperature of 75 °C (167 °F)
- Move mash to lauter tun, then 1 hour rest
- Lauter and sparge with 78 °C (172.4 °F) hot liquor until about 28 litres (7 gal) of wort have been collected
- Add all hops to first runnings

Wort Boil

- Boil wort for 150 minutes

Fermentation

- Chill wort to 8 °C (46.4 °F)
- Add small amount of wort to yeast, after first signs of fermentation pitch yeast
- Ferment at 9 to 10 °C (48.2 to 50 °F)
- Mature and condition in a bunged up and pitched cask for 8 to 10 months; alternatively, you can use a metal keg

Recipe 2 (1870)

- OG 13 °P (1.053)
- 4.2% ABV
- 35 IBU
- 17.4 EBC (8.8 SRM)

Ingredients

- 4.15 kg (8.66 lb) Munich Malt (100%)
- 100 g (3.34 oz) hops, e.g. Hallertauer Mittelfrüh, Saazer or Spalter (3% alpha acid)
- 1 pack bottom-fermenting yeast, e.g. WLP820 or WLP920

Mashing

- Dough in with 19 liters (4.75 gal) of liquor of about 10 °C (50 °F), 3 to 4 hours rest
- Slowly add 7 liters (1.75 gal) of boiling liquor while stirring to increase mash temperature to 33 °C (91.4 °F)
- Draw 10 liters (2.5 gal) of thick mash, bring to a boil, boil for 45 minutes
- Mix back thick mash while stirring, until mash has reached a temperature of 53 °C (127.4 °F), then rest 10 minutes
- Draw 10 liters (2.5 gal) of thick mash, bring to a boil, boil for 45 to 60 minutes
- Mix back thick mash while stirring, until mash has reached a temperature of 65 °C (149 °F), then rest 10 minutes

- Draw 10 liters (2.5 gal) of thin mash, bring to a boil, boil for 30 minutes

- Mix back thin mash while stirring, until mash reached a temperature of 73 °C (163.4 °F)

- Move mash to lauter tun, then rest 1 hour

- Lauter and sparge with 78 °C (172.4 °F) hot liquor until about 26 litres (6.5 gal) of wort have been collected

- Add all hops to first runnings

Wort Boil

- Boil wort for 120 minutes

Fermentation

- Chill wort to 8 °C (46.4 °F)

- Pitch yeast

- Ferment at 9 to 10 °C (48.2 to 50 °F)

- Mature and condition in a bunged up and pitched cask for 8 to 10 months; alternatively, you can use a metal keg

6.3 Munich Winterbier

Unlike Sommerbier, the Winterbier was brewed during the brewing season for quick consumption during that same winter period. That meant that the beer was lighter in original gravity and alcohol, was less hopped employing inferior hops that were up to 3 years old, and was lagered for only a short period of time[5, p.28]. It still had to be at least 6 weeks old from the day it was brewed before it could be served to customers[65, p.58], and if brewed well, it was expected to keep for 5 months or even longer[48, p.215]. The production process is very similar to regular lager beer, though.

Compared to Sommerbier, Winterbier was put into casks earlier, and was kept in the cellar slightly bunged up. This led to a more intense secondary fermentation which was pushing out on the sides of the bung. This usually lasted up to eight days, after which the beer was clear and ready to consume. To improve its quality even more, it was still lagered for another four weeks[33, p.298].

Since the Winterbier was fermented and matured quickly and also quickly consumed during winter, casks were not treated with as much cleanliness as for lager beer: Winterbier casks were often not pitched, but only washed with hot water. New wooden casks were treated with crushed juniper berries and hot water to prevent wood flavour from leeching into the beer[58, p.121].

Recipe (1834)

- OG 14.25 °P (1.058)
- 4.6% ABV
- 23 IBU
- 18.7 EBC (9.5 SRM)

Ingredients

- 4.6 kg (9.6 lb) Munich Malt (100%)
- 63 g (2.1 oz) Bavarian hops, e.g. Hallertauer Mittelfrüh (3% alpha acid); alternatively Saaz hops
- 1 pack bottom-fermenting yeast, e.g. WLP820 or WLP920

Mashing

- Mash, lauter and sparge like Munich Lagerbier from 1834
- Collect only 26 litres (6.5 gal) of wort

Wort Boil

- Boil wort for 90 minutes

Fermentation

- Ferment the same as Munich Lagerbier, but reduce the lagering time to 35 to 40 days

6.4 Bamberger Lagerbier

Beer culture in Bamberg is nowadays often associated with Rauchbier, a more or less smoky lager beer. In historical sources about 19th century beer from Bamberg, there is no mention about a distinct smokiness of the local beer. What is instead highlighted is a very fine flavour, apparently coming from the very gentle mashing regime, a type of infusion mash[35, pp.7-8], or according to some sources a single-decoction mashing process with wort instead of thin mash used for the only decoction[41, pp.119-120]. The Bamberg approach was sometimes even compared to English mashing[39, p.265]. The hops were also treated differently: a separate "roasting" of the hops with a small amount of wort was conducted[35, p.11], which gave the beer a unique flavour[39, p.266]. Both the mash and the hop boil distinguished the Bamberg beers from other Bavarian beers. Not everyone agreed with this approach, though: some brewers preferred to boil the hops as normal, as they found that roasting produced a vegetable-like flavour and an unpleasant bitterness[35, p.64]. Philipp Heiß, former brewmaster at Spaten, mentions that hop roasting has advantages with old and slightly mouldy hops, as it allegedly drives off the harshness and the mouldy smell of the hops[23].

Another technique that is specific to Bamberg is that the wooden casks were not pitched, but burnt on the inside with sulphur instead[35, p.91][41, p.121]. Also unique to Bamberg is unbunged beer, "ungespundet" in German. While lager beer casks in the rest of Bavaria were usually bunged up towards the end of fermentation, in Bamberg the bungholes were only covered with sheets of slate[41, p.121]. The lager beer in Bamberg was bottom-fermented, as only a slow and cold fermentation could prevent possible souring when the beer casks were not bunged. Top-fermented Schenkbier was generally not produced as unbunged beer. Some brewers also added a small amount of salt to the boiling wort as finings, but this would cause thirst and headaches for people that weren't used to it[33, p.326].

Another specialty for Bamberg was the production of Nachbier, a small beer made from sparging the mostly spent malt with either boiling hot or cold liquor, and boiling and fermenting this wort like regular beer. The resulting drink was named Heinzele[33, p.262] or Hainslein[66, p.26].

Recipe 1 (1831/1854)

- OG 12.5 °P (1.050)
- 5% ABV
- 32 IBU
- 18.7 EBC (9.5 SRM)

Ingredients

- 4.6 kg (9.6 lb) Munich malt (100%)
- 83 g (2.77 oz) Spalter hops (3% alpha acid)
- 1 pack bottom-fermenting yeast, e.g. WLP820 or WLP920

Mashing

- Dough in malt in 12 litres (3 gal) of liquor of 68 °C (154.4 °F), so that resulting mash has temperature of 62 °C (143.6 °F), then rest 30 minutes
- Slowly heat up mash to 75 °C (167 °F), then rest 60 minutes
- Start lautering
- Collect 2 litres (0.5 gal) of first runnings, and boil them with all the hops for 30 minutes

- Meanwhile, continue lautering, and sparge with 78 °C hot liquor until a total of about 28 litres (7 gal) of wort are collected

Wort Boil

- When hops have boiled for 30 minutes, add the remaining wort
- Boil for an additional 2 hours

Fermentation

- Chill wort to 8 °C (46.4 °F)
- Add small amount of wort to yeast, after first signs of fermentation pitch yeast
- Ferment at 9 to 10 °C (48.2 to 50 °F)
- Mature and condition in a bunged up cask for up to 10 months; alternatively, you can use a metal keg

Recipe 2 (1818)

- OG 14.5 °P (1.059)
- 5.2% ABV
- 36 IBU
- 22 EBC (11.1 SRM)

Ingredients

- 5.4 kg (11.3 lb) Munich malt (100%)
- 175 g (5.8 oz) Saazer or Spalter hops (3% alpha acid)
- 1 pack bottom-fermenting yeast, e.g. WLP820 or WLP920

Mashing

- Dough in malt in 7 litres (1.75 gal) of liquor of 38 °C (100.4 °F), then rest 15 minutes
- Add 12 litres (3 gal) of liquor of 66 °C (150.8 °F), stir for 15 minutes, then rest 60 minutes
- Start lautering and recirculate wort until it is clear, then completely lauter all wort (first runnings)
- Add 13 litres (3.25 gal) of liquor of 74 °C (165.2 °F), stir for 15 minutes, then rest 60 minutes
- Start lautering and recirculate wort until it is clear, then completely lauter all wort (second runnings)

Wort Boil

- Combine first and second runnings
- Boil all hops with 2 litres (0.5 gal) of wort for 60 minutes, then drain hops
- Add hopped wort to remaining wort, boil for 90 minutes

Fermentation

- Chill wort to 12 °C (53.6 °F)
- Pitch yeast
- Ferment at 12 °C (53.6 °F)
- Mature and condition in a bunged up cask for up to 10 months; alternatively, you can use a metal keg

Variations In the original source to this recipe[66, p.9], the author briefly mentions the use of air-dried malt instead of kilned, dark barley malt. You can therefore substitute the Munich malt with a malt like Pilsner malt or an even paler lager malt.

In order to produce Heinzele, a small beer, pour boiling liquor over the spent grains to collect 13 litres (3.25 gal) of wort. Boil this wort for 60 minutes with the drained hops, then chill the wort to 18 °C (64.4 °F), pitch yeast, and ferment at room temperature.

Bamberger Schenkbier

In Bamberg, not only lager beers were brewed, but also Schenkbier, beer that was brewed in a top-fermenting fashion and could be served relatively quickly without requiring an extended cold maturation phase[33, p.325][41, p.120][26, p.54]. Brewers in Bamberg were not particularly fond of using top-fermenting yeast, and rather preferred bottom-fermenting yeast, so top-fermenting yeast was only used when no other yeast was available. Often brewers on the country-side started brewing earlier than the brewers in Bamberg themselves, and would therefore supply them with fresh bottom-fermenting yeast[66, p.43].

Recipe (1831/1854)

- OG 12.5 °P (1.050)
- 5.4% ABV
- 8 IBU
- 17 EBC (8.6 SRM)

Ingredients

- 4.6 kg (9.6 lb) Munich malt (100%)
- 21 g (0.7 oz) Spalter hops (3% alpha acid)
- 1 pack top-fermenting yeast, e.g. WLP029

Mashing

- Mash, lauter, and sparge like Bamberger Lagerbier

Wort Boil

- Boil like Bamberger Lagerbier

Fermentation

- Chill wort to 20 °C (68 °F)
- Pitch yeast
- After the end of the fermentation, mature and condition beer for 3 to 6 weeks

6.5 Augsburger Lagerbier

The main difference of Augsburger beer lies in the process of how it was made: instead of following the typical Bavarian decoction mash, historic sources describe a unique method that was only practiced in this form in Augsburg.

In addition to the different approach to mashing, the beer was also treated differently when filled into casks: as in other parts of Bavaria, the wooden casks in Augsburg were pitched. But while in other regions the pitch was allowed to cool down, in Augsburg the beer was filled into the casks when the pitch is still burning hot. This was said to give the beer of Augsburg its peculiar flavour that distinguished it from the rest of Bavaria[5, pp.29-31].

Recipe (1834)

- OG 14 °P (1.057)
- 4.9% ABV
- 51 IBU
- 18.4 EBC (9.3 SRM)

Ingredients

- 4.5 kg (9.4 lb) Munich malt (100%)
- 140 g (4.67 oz) Spalter hops (3% alpha acid)
- 1 pack bottom-fermenting yeast, e.g. WLP820 or WLP920

Mashing

- N.B. mashing is best done in a mash tun with a false bottom
- Grind malt finely
- Dough in malt with 6 litres (1.5 gal) of cold liquor of 10 °C (50 °F), rest for 6 hours
- Draw off 0.6 litres (0.15 gal) of wort
- Slowly add about 10 litres (2.5 gal) of boiling liquor under constant stirring, until mash reaches 60 °C (140 °F)
- Remove about 3.5 litres (0.87 gal) of mash and mix with previously drawn-off wort, set aside
- Rest for 2 hours
- Lauter main mash, collect and chill wort
- Bring mash that you set aside earlier to a boil, mix in with main mash, until mash reaches 67 °C (152.6 °F)
- Bring main mash to a boil, boil for 45 minutes, then return to mash tun and let it cool down to 86 °C (186.8 °F)
- Add chilled wort to the copper
- Lauter and sparge main mash with 78 °C (172.4 °F) hot liquor until you've collected about 26 litres (6.5 gal) of wort in the copper

Hop boil

- Bring wort to a boil
- Add all hops to the wort
- Boil hops for 120 minutes

Fermentation

- Chill wort to 8 °C (46.4 °F)

- Pitch yeast

- Wait until fermentation has completed

- Mature and condition in a bunged up and pitched cask for at least 2 months up to 18 months; alternatively, you can use a metal keg

6.6 Salvatorbier

The Salvatorbier draws its origin from a strong beer that used to be brewed in the brewery of a Munich monastery. It was a very seasonal beer, and used to be only served for six days every year in the beginning of April. In the 19th century, this beer was exclusively brewed by Zacherlsches Brauhaus, which was founded in 1813 in the old monastery brewery that had been abandoned in 1799. In 1848, the monopoly on Salvatorbier was lifted, and other breweries were allowed to brew this type of strong beer[39, p.260].

Due to its high gravity of 17.5 to 18.5%, Salvator was an absolute luxury beer, and only the best ingredients like malted barley matured for at least 3 months, and Saazer hops from Bohemia were used[39, p.261].

By the end of the 19th century, several other Munich breweries also brewed Salvatorbier. The brewery, which had been taken over by F.X. Zacherl's nephews, wasn't particularly happy about the competition and their use of the beer name that used to be exclusive to the Zacherl brewery, so they applied for the "Salvator" brand in 1896. This application was subsequently granted in 1899, despite other brewers pleading that "Salvator" was nowadays a generic name that simply described the beer style of dark Doppelbock beer[38, pp.57-60].

The former Zacherl brewery was subsequently renamed to be called "Paulaner-Salvator-Brauerei". Since other breweries were not allowed to use the "Salvator" name for their Salvatorbier anymore, the use of the "-ator" suffix to indicate the style of a Doppelbock became popular, with beers such as "Maximator", "Celebrator", or "Triumphator".

The very limited availability of the beer apparently also led to excessive drinking and everything that comes with it. In April 1841, the "Regensburger Zeitung" newspaper wrote that a fight had broken out at the Zacherl brewhouse between two men apparently very drunk of Salvator. A student and a non-commissioned officer got into an argument, which soon turned violent, with more people joining in, and eventually culminating in other soldiers using their bayonets to injure and mutilate civilians involved in the mass brawl. Because of this huge fight amongst drunk people, the Salvatorbier was criticised as too strong and too cheap as it could turn humans into beasts[1].

Recipe (1854)

- OG 18.5 °P (1.076)
- 6.7% ABV
- 41 IBU
- 24.9 EBC (12.6 SRM)

Ingredients

- 7 kg (14.6 lb) Munich malt (100%)
- 135 g (4.5 oz) Saazer hops (3% alpha acid)
- 1 pack bottom-fermenting yeast, e.g. WLP820 or WLP920

Mashing

- Mash, lauter and sparge like Munich Lagerbier
- Collect only 26 litres (6.5 gal) of wort

Wort Boil

- Boil wort for 90 minutes

Fermentation

- Ferment the same as Munich Lagerbier, but reduce the lagering time to 3 months

6.7 Oktoberfest-Märzenbier

When it comes to beer culture in Munich, probably nothing is more iconic than the Oktoberfest, a huge fair mostly centred around drinking beer in large tents, oompah music, and wearing traditional Bavarian Lederhosen and Dirndln. The roots of this festival were more regal though, as it started as wedding celebrations of the Bavarian Crown Prince Ludwig I. and Princess Therese in 1810. Over the years, it became an annual fair with horse racing, prize shooting, and all kinds of other attractions. Of course, beer was served as well, and this favourite pastime of the citizens of Munich eventually took over the festivities.

In 1872, Michael Schottenhamel was looking for beer to sell at his Oktoberfest tent. Due to an unusually hot summer, most of the Sommerbier was already gone, and since he didn't want to serve Winterbier, Schottenhamel approached Josef Sedlmayr of Franziskaner-Leistbräu. Sedlmayr told him that they've currently got a stronger beer available, brewed in Viennese style, and that it should be in prime condition for Oktoberfest. Schottenhamel agreed to buy the beer, but also announced that he'd sell it for 12 Kreuzer.

12 Kreuzer at that time was the same price as for Salvatorbier, and since beer prices were heavily regulated at that time, the police agreed to allow a probationary sale, which proceeded peacefully, and thus, a more permanent permission was granted. The beer was subsequently advertised as Oktoberfest-Märzenbier, and became the common beer style to be served at the Oktoberfest[56].

The historic source is not entirely clear on the strength of the beer: it mentions Märzen at 16% original gravity, but does not state whether it refers to Märzen in 1872 or 1932. In any case we can derive the likely amount of extract: around the 1870's, the original gravity of Sommerbier was between 13.25 and 15.5%. If we assume that the Märzen was stronger than regular Sommerbier, but less so than Salvatorbier (otherwise the price of 12 Kreuzer would have never been a concern), the original gravity was most likely at 16%. Other than that, the beer brewed was very much like a stronger Vienna lager, probably with an adjusted hopping rate.

Recipe

- OG 16 °P (1.065)
- 6.1% ABV
- 33 IBU
- 10 EBC (5 SRM)

Ingredients

- 5.2 kg (10.8 lb) Vienna malt (100%)
- 100 g (3.34 oz) Saazer hops (3% alpha acid)
- 1 pack bottom-fermenting yeast, e.g. WLP820 or WLP920

Mashing

- Mash, lauter and sparge like Munich Lagerbier
- Collect only 26 litres (6.5 gal) of wort

Wort Boil

- Boil wort for 90 minutes

Fermentation

- Ferment the same as Munich Lagerbier, lager for 6 months

Chapter 7

German White Beers

In Central and Northern Germany, a number of white beers were popularised that were brewed from air-dried malt only. They were usually brewed from a mix of barley malt, wheat malt, and sometimes oat malt, but in some instances, also from barley malt only. They shared commonalities also in other properties: due to the air-dried malt used in the grist, and rather gentle mashing regimes, and sometimes even the lack of a boil gave them a very pale colour, straw-yellow or even white, often with a haze. They were also often described as slightly sour, having wine-like qualities. Very little to no hops were used, so there were was practically no bitterness in these beers.

The earliest known and well-documented example of this group of beer styles is Broyhan, a slightly sour white beer that was brewed since the 16th century and became well-known in large parts of Germany. In some historic literature, it is even seen as a separate category of beer, or as a generic term for all white beers made from wheat[70, p.190], which makes it the archetypal white sour beer in Germany.

Other local beer styles, like Gose and Kottbusser beer, shared a lot of similarities with Broyhan, and were even described to be "like

Broyhan" or even "essentially a kind of Broyhan". Kottbusser Bier in particular also influenced Berliner Weisse, as the yeast from the production of Kottbusser Bier was harvested and shipped to Berlin for Weisse brewers. One source[45, p.76] also mentions that Broyhan was brewed in Berlin, while another one [42, p.10] mentions "Breyhan" as a synonym for the white beer brewed there. With these connections between these beer styles that look, smell and taste very similar to each other, it can be argued that Broyhan may have been the prototypical sour white beer, and other German beer styles may have been brewed in its likeness. This is a subject that requires more research and discussion, but would explain the apparent similarity of different local beers from various parts of Germany.

Interestingly, the geographical closeness of the well-known brewing places of Broyhan and Gose also shows a similarity: the area for which Broyhan brewing has been documented spans from Hanover in the North to the area around Gotha in the South, and from Göttingen in the West to Halle in the East. Parts of this area, in particular a band ranging from Hanover to Halle, including Hildesheim, Halberstadt, and Quedlinburg, is in very close promixity to locations in which Gose brewing has been popular, including Goslar, Quedlinburg, Halberstadt, Aschersleben, and Leipzig. This means that there were some places in which both Gose and and Broyhan used to be brewed.

7.1 Berliner Weisse

Berliner Weisse is the classic top-fermented beer style associated with the city of Berlin. It has been brewed for several hundred years in Berlin itself, and is said to have been praised as "champagne of the north" (Champagne du Nord) by the French military or even "champagne amongst all beers". It is rather unique, and has been described as straw-coloured, similar to wine "from the Rhine", sparkling, with a very dense, almost soapy foam, and of course slightly sour or sometimes sweet-sour. It was usually brewed from varying amounts of air-dried barley malt and wheat malt, occasionally also with small amounts of oat malt to allow for easier lautering[60, p.199]. Only its short shelf life is what brewers in the 19th century considered to be a fault of the beer: in summer, the beer was fine only for about 14 days, in winter about 3 weeks, before it took on too much vinegar-like sourness. The brewers themselves didn't have full control over the brewing process: shortly after fermentation had started, the beer was filled into casks and sent out to innkeepers and beer wholesalers where the fermentation would complete[48, p.192]. There, the beer was also sometimes diluted with water and was eventually bottled and sold. In fact, Berliner Weisse was almost exclusively sold in bottles to customers, and could rarely be found to be served from cask[60, p.201]. The water used for brewing Berliner Weisse was reportedly soft, unlike normal well water in Berlin, and was often taken from the river Spree[60, p.199] [25, p.225].

Berliner Weisse used to get fined, as local beer drinkers expected nothing but a clear beer[63, p.67]. It is also reported to have been brewed from smoked wheat malt for some time, and therefore may at some point have had a smoky flavour[63, p.68].

At least in the first half of the 20th century, Berliner Weisse got its slightly sour character from a mixed fermentation of Saccharomyces (brewers yeast), lactic acid bacteria (in particular Lactobacillus brevis), and Brettanomyces. It is not entirely clear whether it was the same in the centuries before, but sources indicate that the yeast used for fermentation was often either shipped from Cottbus to Berlin as it eventually made the beer too sour if it was repitched more than twice[63, p.67], or that brewers had to buy back yeast from the beer wholesalers. Since Kottbusser Bier was also known as a slightly sour beer, the source of Cottbus for the yeast and the practice of repitching the yeast may have brought this character into the Berliner Weisse. At some point, the mixed yeast/lactobacillus culture must have changed in character and become more stable, as later in the 19th century breweries were repitching their own yeast without the need to regularly replace it, probably in the 1830's or 1840's[63, p.68].

At the height of the beer's popularity, it is said to have been brewed in up to 200 local breweries all over the city, but over the course of the 19th century, its popularity went down, especially due to the success of Bavarian and Bohemian lager beer styles that were either imported or brewed locally in Berlin. In the beginning of the 20th century, only a few large breweries remained that had specialised in brewing just top-fermented beers or even exclusively Berliner Weisse.

As late as the middle of the 20th century, Berliner Weisse was produced as a no-boil beer. The wort was heated up in order to sterilise the wort, even though an increased risk of the beer getting "ropy" remained. When beer got "ropy", it was infected with Pediococcus bacteria, which made the beer syrupy or sometimes even formed slimy strings. Brewers could only get rid of it by maturing the beer, as the consistency eventually changed back to a fully liquid state and the resulting beer got a fine sour aroma that was appreciated by connoisseurs of the beer style.

Around that time, the nature of the mixed fermentation in that it involved both Saccharomyces and Lactobacillus was understood, as well as the necessary maturation temperatures to control the souring of the beer. The beer was bottled right at the end of fermentation, still with some unfermented extract left, and then left to mature between 6 weeks to 3 months. At maturation temperatures of 5 to 6 °C, souring was essentially interrupted, while at 12 to 15 °C, souring progressed a lot quicker and made the beer ready to be consumed more quickly[16, p.16].

Beside the regular Schankbier version of Berliner Weiße with 7 to 8 °P original gravity, stronger versions of the beer was also produced, such as Märzen-Weiße at 12 to 14 °P [63, p.88], or even a Starkbier (strong beer) version with an OG of 16 °P or more [16, p.3]. These stronger versions were matured in the bottle for several months up to several years to develop a wine-like aroma and flavour, and were prized drinks.

Over the course of the century, and with the division of the city after World War II, the few remaining Berliner Weisse breweries were further consolidated, and especially in West Berlin, production processes were rationalised: instead of mixed fermentation, some breweries split up the fermentation process between a "regular" Saccharomyces fermentation and a lactic acid fermentation using Lactobacillus, and to later blend these two. Brettanomyces was left out, as it was hard to control and a common source of beer infections in production facilities that didn't exclusively focus on Berliner Weisse. Due to this rationalisation in production, Berliner Weisse lost much of its character. Another method which would nowadays be called "kettle souring", was experimented with and patented by O. Francke in 1906 as a means to achieve more uniform souring, but was soon abandoned due to a lack in aroma compared to traditionally brewed Weisse[34, p.70].

Only with the recent craft beer boom in Germany, local breweries got interested in reviving this beer style that has once been very popular. In 2011, Michael Schwab of BrewBaker brewery started brewing a vintage Berliner Weisse, and in 2012, Andreas Bogk with his nano brewery "Bogk Bier" started a crowdfunding campaign to support his effort in saving Berliner Weisse by recultivating Brettanomyces strains contained in 1980's East-Berliner Weisse bottles. Both BrewBaker and Bogk Bier created authentic versions of the beer that were more complex than the only commercially available Weisse at that time, focusing on better flavour and aroma rather than an efficient production process. In 2015, Ulrike Genz also started her own brewery named "Schneeeule" to primarily brew Berliner Weisse.

Recipe 1 (1826)

- OG 11.5 °P (1.046)
- 5% ABV
- 10 IBU
- 6.2 EBC (3.1 SRM)

Ingredients

- 2.8 kg (5.8 lb) Pilsner Malt (60.2%)
- 1.5 kg (3.1 lb) Pale Wheat Malt (32.3%)
- 0.35 kg (0.73 lb) Oat Malt (7.5%)
- 32 g (1.07 oz) German hops, e.g. Hallertauer Mittelfrüh (3% alpha acid)
- 1 pack of top-fermenting yeast, e.g. White Labs WLP029
- 1 pack of Lactobacillus, e.g. White Labs WLP672
- Optionally: 1 pack of Brettanomyces, e.g. White Labs WLP645 or WLP650

Mashing

- Dough in with 14 litres (3.5 gal) of liquor at 43 °C (109.4 °F), 30 minutes rest

- Heat up mash to 67 °C (152.6 °F), 1 hour rest
- Pull 4 litres (1 gal) of thin mash, add hops, boil mash for 1 hour
- Add thin mash back to the remaining mash, rest for 1 hour or until iodine test is negative for starch
- Lauter and sparge with 78 °C (172.4 °F) hot liquor
- Collect wort directly in fermentation vessel until about 20 litres (5 gal) are collected
- Optionally: heat wort to 95 °C (203 °F) for 20 minutes to pasteurise it

Fermentation

- Chill wort to 20 °C (68 °F)
- Pitch yeast and Lactobacillus bacteria, optionally also Brettanomyces
- As soon as fermentation has subsided, bottle the young beer

Recipe 2 (1845)

- OG 12 °P (1.048)
- 5.1% ABV
- 7 IBU
- 6.6 EBC (3.3 SRM)

Ingredients

- 3.85 kg (8 lb) Pale Wheat Malt (87.5%)
- 0.55 kg (1.15 lb) Pilsner Malt (12.5%)
- 34 g (1.1 oz) German hops, e.g. Hallertauer Mittelfrüh (3% alpha acid)
- 1 pack of top-fermenting yeast, e.g. White Labs WLP029
- 1 pack of Lactobacillus, e.g. White Labs WLP672
- Optionally: 1 pack of Brettanomyces, e.g. White Labs WLP645 or WLP650

Mashing

- Dough in with 9 litres (2.25 gal) of liquor at 45 °C (113 °F), 30 minutes rest
- Slowly add about 6 litres (1.5 gal) of boiling liquor until the mash has reached a temperature of 67 °C (152.6 °F), then rest for 60 minutes
- Lauter and sparge with 78 °C (172.4 °F) hot liquor until about 24 litres (6 gal) of wort have been collected

Wort Boil

- Add hops to first wort
- Boil wort for 20 minutes

Fermentation

- Chill wort to 22 °C (71.6 °F)
- Pitch yeast and Lactobacillus bacteria, optionally also Brettanomyces
- As soon as fermentation has subsided, bottle the young beer

Recipe 3 (1947)

- OG 8 °P (1.032)
- 3.3% ABV
- 2 IBU
- 5 EBC (2.5 SRM)

Ingredients

- 1.9 kg (3.97 lb) Pilsner Malt (65.5%)
- 1 kg (2.08 lb) Pale Wheat Malt (34.5%)
- 6 g (0.2 oz) German hops, e.g. Hallertauer Mittelfrüh (3% alpha acid)
- 1 pack of top-fermenting yeast, e.g. White Labs WLP029
- 1 pack of Lactobacillus, e.g. White Labs WLP672
- Optionally: 1 pack of Brettanomyces, e.g. White Labs WLP645 or WLP650

Mashing

- Dough in with 9 litres (2.25 gal) of liquor at 30 °C (86 °F), add all hops to mash
- Slowly heat to 54 °C (129.2 °F), rest 30 minutes
- *Very* slowly heat to 75 °C (167 °F) over the course of an hour
- Keep at 75 °C (167 °F) until conversion is complete
- Move one third of the mash to the lauter tun
- Boil the remaining mash for 30 minutes
- Mix boiled mash into lauter tun and let mash settle for 40 minutes in mash tun
- Lauter and sparge with 78 °C (172.4 °F) hot liquor until about 20 litres (5 gal) of wort are collected

Wort Boil

- Heat wort to 95 °C (203 °F) for 20 minutes, but do not bring it to a boil

Fermentation

- Chill wort to 18 °C (64.4 °F)
- Pitch yeast and Lactobacillus bacteria, optionally also Brettanomyces

7.2   Broyhan

Broyhan, sometimes also spelled Broihan or Breihan, is an old white beer named after its inventor, a man named Conrad, Cord, Gerd, Gard or Curd Broyhan, Broihan, or Breihan. Cord Broyhan originally came from Gronau in Lower Saxony, and worked as a brewing labourer in Hamburg, where he learned how to brew Hamburger Bier. He moved to Stöken near Hanover, where he attempted to brew this beer style, which, according to legends, came out differently than planned. He simply decided to sell it as his own beer style which soon became known under his name, Broyhan. Brewing operations soon moved to Hanover, his beer quickly became popular beyond the city and spread to other places and breweries, such as Halberstadt, Quedlinburg, Wolfenbüttel, and Hildesheim[33, p.331].

What made Broyhan unique was that it was a slightly sour white beer that was brewed completely without any hops[48, p.198]. It was relatively low in alcohol, and didn't keep for very long: 14 days in summer [48, p.200], 24 days in winter[33, p.331]. It was known that the ommission of hops gave the beer a sweeter flavour, but at the same time made it more susceptible to going off, which was well-known to beer drinkers at that time[60, p.198].

Other than the lack of hops, its ingredients vary a lot depending on the source: some brewers reported making it from air-dried barley malt only, while others made it from two thirds air-dried barley malt and one third air-dried wheat malt, or about the same amount of barley malt as wheat malt[30, p.150]. Some brewers even used certain amounts of unmalted barley or wheat, but this turned out to be impractical[60, p.197]. In any case, the real Broyhan was described as very pale, both sweet and sour, and an aroma similar to wine.

In March and October, a stronger version, the Doppeltbroyhan, was brewed from the first runnings[28, p.199].

At least at the end of the eighteenth century, brewers in the Electorate of Hanover were also allowed to make vinegar from leftover Broyhan[43, p.238]. In practice, most brewers didn't keep the vessels to produce vinegar, and instead sold leftover Broyhan to brewers that were specialised vinegar producers[43, p.239].

Recipe (1831)

- OG 10.5 °P (1.042)
- 4.1% ABV
- 0 IBU
- 5.5 EBC (2.8 SRM)

Ingredients

- 3.9 kg (8.14 lb) Pilsner malt (100%)
- 1 pack top-fermenting yeast, e.g. WLP029
- 1 pack Lactobacillus delbrueckii, e.g. Wyeast 4335

Mashing

- Dough in malt with 8 litres (2 gal) of liquor at 37 °C (98.6 °F), rest for 30 minutes at 34 °C (93.2 °F)
- Slowly add 17 litres (4.25 gal) of nearly boiling liquor and stir to bring mash to 73 °C (163.4 °F), rest until starch is fully converted
- Lauter and sparge with 78 °C (172.4 °F) hot liquor until about 26 litres (6.5 gal) of wort have been collected

Wort Boil

- Boil wort for 60 minutes

Fermentation

- Chill wort to 17 °C (62.6 °F)
- Pitch yeast and Lactobacillus

Variations Instead of using Pilsner malt only, you can split the grist between Pilsner malt and pale wheat malt in ratios like 2:1, 1:1 or 1:2.

7.3 Gose

In recent years, Gose has attracted the interest of both German breweries and adventurous craft brewers around the world. The main places that are commonly associated with the beer style are the cities of Goslar and Leipzig. The beer itself draws its name from the small river Gose which flows through Goslar. Modern Gose stands out through its ingredients: besides malt, hops and water, coriander and salt are also used for brewing it, and therefore Gose is a prime example for a traditional German beer style brewed outside the constraints of the "purity law". But this has not always been like that.

Already at the end of the 17th century, Gose was described to be brewed like Broyhan, made mostly from wheat malt, and of the same strength as Broyhan[30, p.150]. The Gose from Goslar was considered to be the best, and was characterised as having nutritional and laxative properties, which also showed in a number of joke rhymes at that time[33, p.335].

The earliest detailed description how Goslarer Gose was brewed can be found in the book "Epistola Itineraria XXXVIII. De Cerevisia Goslariensi" by Franc. Ern. Brückmann, published in 1735[8]. In this book, Gose is described as brewed from wheat malt exclusively. Its production was rather intricate and involved four separate infusion mashes resulting in four beers of different quality, named "Hopf-Krug", "Allerley-Krug", "Bester Krug" and "Vier-Pfannen-Bier". A small beer named "Kofent" was produced from the spent grains. Besides hops, other spices as well as salt were used. To help with lautering, rye straw and wicker baskets functioning as sieves were used.

Even in 19th century brewing literature, Gose was considered to be a white beer similar to Broyhan[25, p.220], which meant a very pale colour from using air-dried or only lightly kilned wheat and barley malt[60, pp.198-199]. Its flavour could be characterised as having sweetness upfront, followed by a wine-like tartness with no discernible hop aroma or bitterness. These wine-like qualities also made it usable as a substitute for wine in cooking[33, p.335].

Other sources describe Gose as a beer made from 100% wheat malt: Döllnitzer Gose was such a version, which is also described as salty and pleasantly sour. The saltiness came from the use of table salt in the boil[29, p.41]. Analysis data from 1904 shows that the amounts of salt found in Gose were in the range between 0.13 g/L and 0.26 g/L[50].

Originally, Gose from Goslar was a spontaneously fermented beer: it was reported as starting fermentation by itself within 12 to 24 hours[8], during which a thick, leather-like mould pellicle formed on top of it. It may not have been completely spontaneous, though: fermentation vessels, usually wooden vats, were cleaned with hot spruce water, which was most likely not enough to kill off all yeast and bacteria residing in them[51].

Goslarer Gose was usually consumed fresh while it was not sour yet, but at the same time, it did not keep particularly well, and so this beer was very prone to go sour and become vinegar. This meant that the beer had to be sold very quickly. In order to promote quick sales, homebrewing was prohibited in Goslar in January 1826, and in January 1827, a general assembly of the local brewers society was held to discuss whether its members should stop brewing Gose and switch to a brown, more highly hopped beer made from properly kilned malt, either completely or at least during the so-called "sour time", presumably the warm weather periods[11, p.484].

The preference for a fresh, unsoured Gose is also what distinguished the Goslarer Gose from the Leipziger Gose: Gose in Leipzig was stored in open bottles with a long bottleneck and only a small opening. It underwent secondary fermentation which not only gave it a very sharp sourness with a very distinct vinegar note, it also formed a plug of yeast which closed up the bottle. The right moment to consume it had to be watched out for, as young Gose was called "Birnbrühe" (lit. "pear broth"), too old Gose was simply "Essig" (vinegar), while Gose at the right age was described as "Limonade mit Geist" ("lemonade with spirit")[27].

Around 1900, Gose was the most popular beer style in Leipzig, but by the end of World War 2, no more Gose was brewed. Only in 1949, the small brewery Wurzler restarted Gose brewing, but eventually gave up and closed its gates in 1966. Gose as a beer style was functionally extinct, until the Weissbier brewery section of VEB Getränkekombinat Berlin, one of the East German state-owned breweries, started contract-brewing a Gose for the Leipziger café *Ohne Bedenken*. After German reunification, brewing of Gose was also picked up again in Goslar, and with the growth of the craft beer scene world-wide, Gose has become a common beer style for breweries to rebrew and interpret.

Recipe (1831)

- OG 12.5 °P (1.050)
- 5.3% ABV
- 4 IBU
- 6.5 EBC (3.3 SRM)

Ingredients

- 2.5 kg (5.2 lb) Pilsner malt (54.4%)
- 2.1 kg (4.4 lb) pale wheat malt (45.6%)
- 12 g (0.4 oz) German hops, e.g. Hallertauer Mittelfrüh (3% alpha acid)
- 1 pack top-fermenting yeast, e.g. WLP029
- 1 pack Lactobacillus delbrueckii, e.g. Wyeast 4335

Mashing

- Dough in grist with 24 litres (6 gal) of liquor at 47 °C (116.6 °F), so that the resulting mash temperature is 45 °C (113 °F), then rest 1 hour
- Slowly heat up 72 °C (161.6 °F), then rest for 1 hour
- Lauter, sparge with 78 °C (172.4 °F) hot liquor until about 26 litres (6.5 gal) of wort have been collected

Wort Boil

- Boil wort for 60 minutes, add hops at the beginning of the boil

Fermentation

- Chill wort to 18 °C (64.4 °F)
- Pitch yeast and Lactobacillus

Variations Instead of using a mix of Pilsner malt and pale wheat malt, you can use a grist of 100% pale wheat malt. In this case, also use rice hulls or oat husks in the mash to allow for an easier lauter and sparge process.

7.4 Kottbusser Bier

This beer from Cottbus in the German state of Brandenburg is described as being similar to Broyhan, but unlike the Broyhan, hops were employed in its production. An alternative name for this beer is also Kottwitzer Bier, which stems from the medieval name of Cottbus[33, p.337].

Besides the often described similarity to Broyhan, the beer also seems to have been very sparkling and forming a large amount of foam. The beer also most likely was sour to a certain extent, probably just like a Berliner Weisse, and there is strong evidence for this: in fact, Berliner Weisse brewers received regular shippings of yeast from Cottbus well into the 19th century[22, p.228]. Only later in the 19th century, a stable local mixed culture had formed in Berlin so that brewers could repeatedly repitch their own yeast. Before that, the used yeast had to be refreshed, otherwise the brewed Berliner Weisse would have turned out to be too sour.

Original recipes for this beer style are not well known, but several recreations based on more or less reliable sources from the 19th century can be identified in old beer literature. The ingredients often include air-dried malts made from barley, wheat and oats, cane sugar, honey, as well as hops.

Recipe 1 (1845)

- OG 10.5 °P (1.042)
- 4.4% ABV
- 10 IBU
- 5.5 EBC (2.8 SRM)

Ingredients

- 3 kg pale wheat malt (80.2%)
- 0.65 kg oat malt (17.4%)
- 0.09 kg white cane sugar (2.4%)
- 50 g German hops, e.g. Hallertauer Mittelfrüh (3% alpha acid)
- 1 pack top-fermenting yeast, e.g. WLP029
- 1 pack Lactobacillus delbrueckii, e.g. Wyeast 4335

Mashing

- Dough in grist with 7 litres of liquor at 43 °C, so that resulting temperature is 39 °C, then rest 15 minutes
- Slowly mix in 9 litres of boiling water to bring temperature up to 70 °C, rest for 1 hour
- Slowly mix in 6.5 laters of boiling water to bring temperature up to 78 °C
- Take 4 litres of mash, boil with hops for 15 minutes, then slowly mix back to main mash to reach about 80 °C, then rest 1 hour
- Lauter, sparge with 78 °C hot liquor until about 24 litres of wort have been collected

Wort boil

- Boil wort for 30 minutes with cane sugar

Fermentation

- Chill wort to 20 °C
- Pitch yeast and Lactobacillus

Recipe 2 (1831)

- OG 9.5 °P (1.038)
- 3.8% ABV
- 10 IBU
- 5.5 EBC (2.8 SRM)

Ingredients

- 1.95 kg (4.07 lb) pale wheat malt (52%)
- 1.25 kg (2.6 lb) Pilsner malt (33.3%)
- 0.35 kg (0.73 lb) flaked oats (9.3%)
- 0.1 kg (0.2 lb) white cane sugar (2.7%)
- 0.1 kg (0.2 lb) honey (2.7%)
- 28 g (0.9 oz) German hops, e.g. Hallertauer Mittelfrüh (3% alpha acid)
- 1 pack top-fermenting yeast, e.g. WLP029
- 1 pack Lactobacillus delbrueckii, e.g. Wyeast 4335

Mash

- Dough in grist with 7 litres (1.75 gal) of liquor at 50 °C (122 °F), so that resulting temperature is 45 °C (113 °F), rest 15 minutes
- Slowly mix in 7 litres (1.75 gal) of boiling water to bring temperature up to 70 °C (158 °F), rest for 1.5 hours
- Lauter, sparge with 78 °C (172.4 °F) hot liquor until about 26 litres (6.5 gal) of wort have been collected

Wort Boil

- Boil wort for 60 minutes, add hops at the beginning of the boil
- Add white cane sugar and honey at the end of the boil

Fermentation

- Chill wort to 20 °C (68 °F)
- Pitch yeast and Lactobacillus

7.5 Grätzer/Grodziskie

The Polish city of Grätz/Grodzisk Wielkopolski only became part of Prussia in 1793, but already in the 13th century migration from Germany had started. The local beer style has been brewed there for centuries, and was allegedly brought to the city by German colonists in the 15th century[63]. It was brewed exclusively from wheat malt (though some sources mention the use of a certain share of barley malt[32]), and earned a good reputation as a sparkling, refreshing, and spicy drink. Due to its popularity, it started being brewed in other places as well. In Germany, the beer style was brewed well into the 1940's. In 1947, two Berlin breweries, Monopolbrauerei and Hochschulbrauerei, still produced Grätzer/Grodziskie in relatively small amounts[16, p.30], the latter one ceased the production of Grätzer only in the 1970's[2].

The malt was smoked using oak. The resulting beer was naturally hazy, and was thus fined with isinglass. Due to the preservative qualities of the smoke and the hops, Grätzer/Grodziskie was considered to be a beer that wouldn't go off easily and therefore could be matured for a year or longer. Over time, the mature beer developed an aroma that was described as fruit-like[63].

Between the the middle of the 19th century of the early 20th century, the fermentation method of Grätzer/Grodziskie has profoundly changed, though: in 1864, the cold break from the wort was mixed with finely crushed willow bark, and shaped into a loaf which was placed into an empty vat. The next day, the wort was poured on top of this loaf into the vat, and well-mixed. It was then filled into casks and sent out to the pubs. During transportation, the beer started to ferment, and continued to ferment unbunged for 8 more days in the pub cellar. It was then bottled and left to condition for several weeks until it was sparkling. The willow bark was not the cause of the fermentation, though. While it leeched tannines and salicin into the wort, the yeast itself was most likely coming from remains on the inside of the transportation casks[18, p.262].

Because of the smoke-kilning of the malt, it can be argued that Grätzer/Grodziskie is not a "true" white beer despite its pale colour, and that it's technically a brown beer. Even if it's considered a white beer, it certainly distinguishes itself from all other white beers through its pronounced hop bitterness and a total lack of a sour character.

Since 2011, the project "Grodziskie Redivivus" of the Polish Homebrewers Association has been working on researching on rebrewing this beer style. In 2012, they issued a report about their findings on how Grodziskie was brewed and what they consider important in its production, including an example recipe based on their research[53].

Recipe 1 (1902)

- OG 7 °P (1.028)
- 2.9% ABV
- 30 IBU
- 4.7 EBC (2.4 SRM)

Ingredients

- 2.6 kg (5.43 lb) oak smoked wheat malt (100%)
- 70 g (2.34 oz) Polish hops, e.g. Nowotomyski (3% alpha acid); alternatively Polish, Czech, or German noble hops
- 1 pack top-fermenting yeast, e.g. WLP029

Mash

- Dough in with 9 litres (2.25 gal) of liquor at 45 °C (113 °F), 30 minutes rest
- Slowly add about 6 litres (1.5 gal) of boiling liquor until the mash has reached a temperature of 67 °C (152.6 °F), then rest for 60 minutes
- Lauter and sparge with 78 °C (172.4 °F) hot liquor until about 26 litres (6.5 gal) of wort have been collected

Wort Boil

- Boil wort for 60 minutes, add hops at the beginning of the boil

Fermentation

- Chill wort to 15-19 °C (59-66.2 °F)
- Pitch yeast
- After end of fermentation, fine with isinglass (optional)

Recipe 2 (1930)

- OG 8 °P (1.032)
- 3.2% ABV
- 18 IBU
- 5.0 EBC (2.5 SRM)

Ingredients

- 2.15 kg (4.48 lb) oak smoked wheat malt (60.6%)
- 1.1 kg (2.29 lb) Pilsner malt (31%)
- 0.3 kg (0.62 lb) oat husks (8.4%)
- 33 g (1.1 oz) Lublin hops (4% alpha acid)
- 1 pack top-fermenting yeast, e.g. WLP029

Mash

- Dough in malt and oat husks in 10 litres (2.5 gal) of cold liquor, rest for 1 hour
- Take about 1 litre (0.25 gal) from the mash and put it in the lauter tun
- Heat up to 40 °C (104 °F), rest 10 minutes
- Heat up to 56 °C (132.8 °F), rest 20 minutes
- Heat up to 67 °C (152.6 °F), rest 30 minutes
- Heat up to 75 °C (167 °F), rest 60 minutes
- Bring mash to a boil, boil for 60 minutes
- Let mash cool to 75 °C (167 °F)
- Lauter and sparge with 78 °C (172.4 °F) hot liquor until about 26 litres (6.5 gal) of wort have been collected

Wort Boil

- Boil wort for 90 minutes, add hops at the beginning of the boil

Fermentation

- Chill wort to 15 °C
- Pitch yeast
- After end of fermentation, fine with isinglass (optional)

Recipe 3 (2012)

- OG 7.7 °P (1.031)
- 3.1% ABV
- 22 IBU
- 5.0 EBC (2.5 SRM)

Ingredients

- 2.85 kg (5.95 lb) oak smoked wheat malt (100%)
- 29 g (0.97 oz) Lublin hops (5% alpha acid)
- 1 pack top-fermenting yeast, e.g. WLP029

Mash

- Dough in malt with 3.8 litres (0.95 gal) of liquor at 43 °C (109.4 °F) to reach mash temperature of 38 °C (100.4 °F), rest 30 minutes
- Add 2.1 (0.52 gal) litres of liquor at 75 °C (167 °F) to reach mash temperature of 52 °C (125.6 °F), rest 30 to 60 minutes
- Slowly add 4.5 (1.12 gal) litres of boiling liquor over the course of 20 minutes to reach mash temperature of 70 °C (158 °F), rest 30 minutes

- Add 2.3 (0.57 gal) litres of boiling liquor to reach mash temperature of 75 °C (167 °F), then mash out
- Lauter and sparge with 78 °C (172.4 °F) hot liquor until about 26 litres (6.5 gal) of wort have been collected

Wort Boil

- Boil wort for 120 minutes
- Add 23 g (0.77 oz) of hops 105 minutes before end of boil
- Add 6 g (0.2 oz) of hops 30 minutes before end of boil

Fermentation

- Chill wort to 14-16 °C (57.2-60.8 °F)
- Pitch yeast
- After end of fermentation, fine with isinglass (optional)

Chapter 8

German Brown Beers

Brown beer was probably the most prevalent general type of beer in Germany. It was distinguished from white beer through its colour: brown beers were made from kilned malts, which, due to technological limitations of that time, could not be controlled precisely and therefore often produced a relatively dark malt which naturally produced a dark, brown wort.

Outside of Bavaria, most beer was top-fermented, and brown beers were no exception. Because of that, most of them were running beers which were consumed without much maturation since they could spoil easily and go sour. Hop bitterness was usually also more pronounced, often to offset the rich maltiness and in some instances the smokiness from the malt.

In more highly attenuated beers, where there was less of a malty sweetness from residual sugars, the bitterness of the hops often dominated. These beers were sometimes named "Bitterbier" to distinguish them from the sweeter, maltier varieties. The other extreme were nutritious beers like Brunswick Mumme or Danziger Jopenbier, which were brewed not for refreshment or recreational use, but primarily as a nutritional drink with a high sugar content, not unlike modern malt extracts or malt beverages.

Since most of Germany was not governed by Bavarian brewing legislation until the beginning of the 20th century, brown beers were more diverse: not only did brewers use grains other than barley as a starch source, they could also afford to flavour the beer with herbs and fruits other than just hops.

8.1 Berliner Braunbier

Berliner Braunbier, which literally translates to "Berlin brown beer", is another beer style that originated from the Prussian capital. Unlike its white beer cousin Berliner Weisse, Berliner Braunbier has not survived into modern times, and so less is known about this beer style. It was top-fermented and brewed from barley malt only[48, p.193].

The basis of this beer forms a very dark malt, a brown malt dried at high temperatures on a smoke kiln, and was used only 6 months after malting[48, p.194], presumably to lose some of the smokiness. The beer style itself had a relatively bad reputation, as it could be watered down by innkeepers without the customers noticing due to dark colour.

Historically speaking, Berliner Braunbier may have actually been two distinct styles of brown beer. One version was bitter-sweet, which might be an indicator for either a relatively low attenuation or a low hopping rate, while the other one was purely bitter, and was also known as Bitterbier[22, p.275]. It also had a roasty and smoky aroma and flavour, coming from the malt that was dried on smoke kilns[22, p.276]. Although the use of smoke kilns was criticised as obsolescent in the middle of the 19th century, brewers claimed that their customers had gotten used to the smoky beer[22, p.277], and thus feared for their sales in case they changed their kilning process to be smokeless.

There is some indication that Berliner Braunbier may have been a slightly sour beer. Records from 1850[44, p.342] show an acidity of 0.51%, which would be just above the taste perception threshold.

At some point in time, the malt for Berliner Braunbier was produced from a specific variety of barley, so-called four-row barley[22, p.276]. Four-row barley is actually a loose variation of six-row barley, and was allegedly easy to malt.

Just like Berliner Weisse, Berliner Braunbier was sent out to beer wholesalers, victuallers and pubs while it was still actively fermenting, and was usually diluted with water[22, p.281].

In these two reconstructed recipes, the high-dried brown malt was replaced by Munich malt and a certain amount of black malt. Using a less dark malt and some roasted malt to achieve a certain roasted character and a very dark beer colour were improvements to the beer style that were discussed in some of the brewing literature of the 19th century. The described mashing regimes are simplified and slightly modified to ensure a full conversion of all starches in the mash.

Recipe 1 (1845)

- OG 15.5 °P (1.063)
- 6.7% ABV
- 10 IBU
- 47.6 EBC (24.2 SRM)

Ingredients

- 5.6 kg (11.7 lb) Munich malt (96.5%)
- 0.2 kg (0.41 lb) Black malt (3.5%)
- 28 g (0.93 oz) German hops, e.g. Hallertauer Mittelfrüh (3% alpha acid)
- 1 pack of top-fermenting yeast, e.g. White Labs WLP029

Mashing

- Dough in malt in 10 litres (2.5 gal) of liquor of 50 °C temperature (122 °F), rest 30 min
- Add 10 litres (2.5 gal) of boiling liquor to raise temperature to 68 °C (154.4 °F), then rest 90 min
- Draw a thick mash of 6 litres (1.5 gal) and bring to a boil, then mix back to raise temperature to 75 °C (167 °F) and rest for 45 minutes
- Lauter and sparge with 78 °C (172.4 °F) hot liquor until about 26 litres (6.5 gal) of wort have been collected

Wort Boil

- Add all hops to wort, then bring wort to a boil
- Boil for 90 minutes

Fermentation

- Chill wort to 25 °C (77 °F)
- Pitch yeast

Variation: Bitterbier To produce a Bitterbier version of Berliner Braunbier, use 220 g (7.3 oz) of hops. The resulting beer will have about 75 IBU.

Recipe 2 (1826)

- OG 16 °P (1.065)
- 6.9% ABV
- 30 IBU
- 47.9 EBC (24.3 SRM)

Ingredients

- 5.8 kg (12.1 lb) Munich malt (96.7%)
- 0.2 kg (0.41 lb) Black malt (3.3%)
- 87 g (2.9 oz) German hops, e.g. Hallertauer Mittelfrüh (3% alpha acid)
- 1 pack of top-fermenting yeast, e.g. White Labs WLP029

Mashing

- Dough in malt in 9 litres (2.25 gal) of liquor at 72 °C (161.6 °F), the resulting mash should have 61 °C (141.8 °F), then rest 30 minutes
- Slowly mix in 7 litres (1.75 gal) of boiling water, the resulting mash should have 76 °C (168.8 °F), then rest 120 minutes
- Move mash to lauter tun, slowly mix in another 9 litres (2.25 gal) of boiling water
- Lauter and sparge with 78 °C (172.4 °F) hot liquor until about 26 litres (6.5 gal) of wort have been collected

Wort Boil

- Add all hops to wort, then bring wort to a boil
- Boil for 90 minutes

Fermentation

- Chill wort to 23 °C (73.4 °F)
- Pitch yeast

8.2 Fredersdorfer Bier

A former chamberlain of Frederick William I. of Prussia, Michael Gabriel Fredersdorf (or Fredersdorff), first had this beer brewed in the Spandau-based brewery that he owned[25, pp.201-202] [22, p.328]. Between 1825 and 1830, it was one of the most popular beers in Berlin, and was produced both in Spandau and Berlin in large quantities. It was known as very alcoholic, clear, pale brown, and highly carbonated[33, p.332]. Eventually, this beer style was supplanted by the upcoming fashion of Bavarian-style lager beers, but was still brewed later in the mid-19th century and sold as Braun-Bitterbier.

Recipe (1831)

- OG 18.5 °P (1.076)
- 8% ABV
- 48 IBU
- 22.3 EBC (11.3 SRM)

Ingredients

- 3.45 kg (7.2 lb) dark wheat malt (42.4%)
- 2.3 kg (4.8 lb) Munich malt (28.2%)
- 2.3 kg (4.8 lb) Vienna malt (28.2%)
- 0.09 kg (0.19 oz) molasses syrup (1.2%)
- 163 g (5.44 oz) German hops, e.g. Hallertauer Mittelfrüh (3% alpha acid)
- 1 pack top-fermenting yeast, e.g. WLP029

Mashing

- Mash like Berliner Braunbier

Wort Boil

- Add all hops to wort, then bring wort to a boil
- Boil for 90 minutes
- Dissolve molasses after the end of the boil

Fermentation

- Chill wort to 17 °C (62.6 °F)
- Pitch yeast

8.3 Mannheimer Braunbier

This beer style originally comes from the city of Mannheim in the South-Western German state of Baden-Württemberg. It became well-known all over Germany, which led to brewery workers from Mannheim being hired by breweries all over Germany, under the assumption they were some of the best brewers in Germany[60, p.191].

Beer brewing done by brewers from Mannheim is documented for the city of Halle in the eighteenth century[57, p.560]. After Mannheim had been burned down in 1689, a large number of Mannheimers emigrated to Halle. They received the permission to brew the local Mannheim beer style, which became more popular and was prized as much as Merseburger beer, but unlike Merseburger, was a lot less bitter[4, p.69].

The beer brewed in Halle was of golden colour and contained juniper berries[57, p.560]. Mannheimer Bier became especially popular in cities like Berlin, where it was also brewed for some time. There, it was at some point a particularly fashionable beer together with Fredersdorfer Bier, until Bavarian lager beers entered the market and slowly supplanted Mannheimer Braunbier.

Recipe (1831)

- OG 13.5 °P (1.055)
- 5.5% ABV
- 63 IBU
- 15.7 EBC (7.9 SRM)

Ingredients

- 2.75 kg (5.74 lb) Munich malt (50%)
- 2.75 kg (5.74 lb) Vienna malt (50%)
- 180 g (6 oz) Tettnanger hops (3% alpha acid)
- 14 g (0.47 oz) juniper berries
- 4 g (0.13 oz) ginger root (chopped)
- 1 pack top-fermenting yeast, e.g. WLP029

Preparations

- Smash juniper berries and soak them in 1 litre (0.25 gal) of water for 24 hours, then remove berries

Mashing

- Dough in grist with 10 litres (2.5 gal) of liquor of 50 °C (122 °F), then rest for 30 minutes
- Add 10 litres (2.5 gal) of boiling liquor to bring temperature of mash to about 68 °C (154.4 °F), then rest until starch has been completely converted
- Vorlauf until wort is clear
- Draw 1 litre (0.25 gal) of clear wort and boil all hops with it for 15 minutes
- Lauter and sparge with 78 °C (172.4 °F) hot liquor until a total of about 25 litres (6.25 gal) of wort are collected

Hop boil

- Add remaining wort to the boiling wort with the hops

- boil for 90 minutes
- Add juniper berry infusion to wort at the end of the boil

Fermentation

- Chill wort to 20 °C (68 °F)
- Add chopped up ginger to wort
- Pitch yeast

8.4 Braunschweiger Mumme

Braunschweiger Mumme, or Brunswick Mum as it was called in English, was a major beer export article of the German city of Braunschweig (Brunswick) since the end of the 15th century. Allegedly, it was invented by a brewer named Christian Mumme and first brewed in 1492. 19th century literature describe it as dark brown, very thick and almost syrupy, making it more of a nourishing than a refreshing or intoxicating drink. When shipped, its quality allegedly improved through the long journey[68, p.735]. In the 19th century, the popularity of Mumme had already drastically decreased, and it was only produced in small amounts.

In 19th century English brewing literature, Mum is mentioned, but mostly for the large import duty that had been put on it. Also, local imitations are mentioned that also called themselves "Mum" but were brewed in Ireland[5, p.49].

The historicity of Braunschweiger Mumme recipes is difficult. Especially in the 18th and 19th century, a number of recipes circulated, some of them claiming they were based on an official recipe that was kept in the archives of the town hall of Braunschweig. Ultimately, the exact ingredients, recipes and production processes are unknown.

What is known though is that two different versions existed: Stadtmumme, a common drink made for home consumption and low strength, and Schiffsmumme, a higher strength brew made for export.

Recipe (1831)

- OG 24 °P (1.101)
- 8.9% ABV
- 22 IBU

- 32.9 EBC (16.7 SRM)

Ingredients

- 4.35 kg (9.08 lb) dark wheat malt (66.9%)
- 2.15 kg (4.48 lb) Munich malt (33.1%)
- 42 g (1.4 oz) German hops, e.g. Hallertauer Mittelfrüh (3% alpha acid)
- 21 g (0.7 oz) juniper berries
- 2 g (0.06 oz) marjoram
- 2 g (0.06 oz) thyme
- 1 g (0.03 oz) dried elderflowers
- 17 g (0.57 oz) plums
- 1 pack of low-attenuating top-fermenting yeast, e.g. SafBrew S-33

Preparation

- Add hops, juniper berries, marjoram, thyme, elderflowers and plum to 1 litre (0.25 gal) of almost boiling water
- Strain after 10 hours to get extract

Mashing

- Dough in grist with 25 litres (6.25 gal) of liquor at 80 °C (176 °F), then rest 1 hour
- Heat up to 84 °C (183.2 °F),
- Lauter and collect wort

Wort Boil

- Boil wort until it has reduced to about 10 litres (2.5 gal)

Fermentation

- Chill wort to 20 °C (68 °F)
- Add extract to wort
- Pitch yeast

Making Stadtmumme In a historic source from 1690, the ratios between Schiffsmumme and Stadtmumme are listed[30, p.139]. Based on that, you can reduce the malt to 2.8 kg (5.85 lb) dark wheat malt and 1.4 kg (2.92 lb) Munich malt and the hops to only 7 g (0.23 oz), otherwise follow the recipe as described above. You should end up with a beer with an OG of about 15.5 °P (1.063), 5.7% ABV and only about 4 IBU.

Another hypothesis is that Stadtmumme was made from the second wort: after brewing a Schiffsmumme, you can conduct a second mash, lauter and collect the wort, and boil it. Using the spent hops, juniper berries, plums and spices, create a second extract in the same way, and add it after you've chilled the second wort.

8.5 Merseburger Bier

Merseburger Bier was well known around Germany. It is described as having a dark brown colour, good clarity, a bitter-aromatic flavour, and was allegedly very nutritious[33, p.339]. Goethe mentioned it in some of his writing, where he described it as "bitter as the death on the gallows", but also mentions that you get used to it after you've been drinking it for a week[21]. In some literature Merseburger Bier is mentioned as a beer that is matured for an extended period of time, most likely several months, until it was consumed[52, p.184].

As a highly bittered beer, it was known as more stable and less perishable than other beers, which is why it was a common export beer. In particular cities like Halle and Leipzig, which had no good local beer due to poor water quality, it was imported in large amounts in the eighteenth century[4, p.66]. As late as 1823, Merseburger Bier was considered to be one of the best brown beers in Germany, but the slow downfall was already noticeable: of formerly four brew houses in Merseburg, only a single one was still brewing beer[4, p.91].

Recipe (1826)

- OG 16.5 °P (1.068)
- 6.2% ABV
- 125 IBU
- 18.2 EBC (9.2 SRM)

Ingredients

- 3.5 kg (7.3 lb) Munich malt (57.1%)

- 2.63 kg (5.49 lb) Vienna malt (42.9%)
- 400 g (13.36 oz) German hops, e.g. Hallertauer Mittelfrüh (3% alpha acid)
- 20 g (0.67 oz) gentian root
- 8 g (0.27 oz) dried green bitter orange
- 1 pack top-fermenting yeast, e.g. WLP029

Preparations

- Infuse gentian root and dried bitter orange in 1 litre (0.25 gal) of hot water for 24 hours, then strain.

Mashing

- Dough in with 25 litres of liquor at 66 °C (150.8 °F). The resulting mash temperature should be 62 °C (143.6 °F). Rest 1 hour.
- Heat up mash to 75 °C (167 °F), rest 1 hour.
- Lauter and sparge with 78 °C (172.4 °F) hot liquor until about 26 litres (6.5 gal) of wort have been collected

Wort Boil

- Add all hops to wort, then bring wort to a boil
- Boil for 90 minutes

Fermentation

- Chill wort to 20 °C (68 °F)
- Add gentian root and bitter orange infusion to wort
- Pitch yeast

Chapter 9

Historic Austrian Beer

Even though Austria certainly had a rich beer culture, it is not as well-documented as, for example, German beer culture of the same time. If you expand the term "Austria" to not only include what constitutes Austria today, but also the Habsburger's inherited land in the Holy Roman Empire, and later the Austrian empire respectively the Cisleithanian part of the Austrian-Hungarian empire, you do get an area with a rich beer history and great influence on the global emergence of lager beer brewing, in particular Lower Austria including Vienna and its contributions to industrial lager brewing; Bohemia, which was one of Europe's largest hop producing regions and where the worldwide revolution of pale lager beers started; Carinthia, where an old tradition of Austrian farmhouse brewing survived until the early 20th century; and Styria including parts of what is nowadays Slovenia, which still forms a relatively important European hop growing region.

Some of the historic Austrian beer styles are only known by name or by very vague descriptions. In the 19th century, Regensburger Bier, a pitch-black, top-fermented beer, was very popular, then there was Mailänder Bier (the name is alluding to the Italian city of Milan) which was paler than Regensburger but not particularly clear. The so-called Luftbier ("air beer") was also popular, as well as Horner Bier, a unique oat ale of which a recipe can be found in this book.

Already at the beginning of the 19th century, old local beer styles had disappeared, and the Austrian beer market was dominated by Bavarian and English-style beers. In other regions, in particular Carinthia and Styria, an old farmhouse stone beer brewing tradition remained alive until the beginning of the 20th century. This can possibly be seen as one of the last artefacts of medieval brewing methods that survived into the modern age.

In the second half of the 19th century, Austria played a more important role in the revolution of worldwide beer culture: Vienna and Pilsen/Plzeň were the first places where pale, bottom-fermented lager beers where brewed, which, in combination with the industrialisation of beer brewing as such, caught on as an international standard for beer production. Within just a few decades, almost all brewers started imitating pale lagers, especially those of the Pilsner style, and nowadays the largest share of internationally produced beer is pale, bottom-fermented lager beer.

9.1 Horner Bier

Horner Bier is an extinct beer style from the Lower Austrian city of Horn that was popular in Austria in the 18th and 19th century, in particular in Vienna. Some sources claim that it was invented by a brew master named Faber in 1750, who held an exclusive privilege to produce this particular type of beer until his death[59]. In fact, Horner Bier is already mentioned in a resolution by Austrian Arch Duke Leopold V regarding the taxation of beer from 1687[10, p.221].

By 1835, brewing in Horn had stopped[59]. In Vienna, Horner Bier was produced in small quantities in the brew house of Margareten[6].

Horner Bier was brewed exclusively from oat malt, and because of that, was rather murky, with a very pale, yellow-green colour. It was also described as very fizzy. According to some sources, cream of tartar was added to the wort to get a slightly sour and refreshing flavour. Even Mozart mentions this beer in his canon "Bei der Hitz im Sommer eß ich" (K. 234/382e) as a refreshing summer drink[31].

Unfortunately, no information has been preserved about original gravity, alcohol content or production method, so this recipe is an interpretation of the rather vague descriptions of the beer itself.

Recipe

- OG 8.5 °P (1.034)
- 3.6% ABV
- 10 IBU
- 5.9 EBC (3 SRM)

Ingredients

- 4 kg (8.35 lb) oat malt (100%)
- 20 g (0.67 oz) Saazer hops (4% alpha acid)
- 10 g (0.33 oz) cream of tartar
- 1 pack top-fermenting yeast, e.g. WLP029

Mashing

- Dough in with 12 litres (3 gal) of liquor at 67 °C (152.6 °F), rest until fully converted
- Lauter and sparge with 78 °C (172.4 °F) hot liquor until about 26 litres have been collected
- Add all hops to wort

Wort Boil

- Bring wort to boil
- Dissolve cream of tartar at the beginning of the boil in the wort

Fermentation

- Chill wort to 20 °C (68 °F)
- Pitch yeast

9.2 Carinthian Stone Beer

Stone beer is a type of beer that within Austria was popular in Carinthia and Styria. It can be made with the simplest of tools and is fermented raw (i.e. unboiled), which indicates that this may have been the remnants of a much older brewing tradition possibly going back to the middle ages. The use of stones grew out of the limitation that large kettles were either too expensive or too impractical to build, so mashing was done in simple wooden tubs. Hot stones, heated up in a fire of cherry wood[9, p.10], were used to heat up the mash, and the resulting wort was not boiled[69].

Carinthian stone beer ("Kärntner Steinbier" in German) in its original form was apparently an oat beer, but in the 19th century, parts of the oats were replaced by barley and later by barley and wheat. Because of the simple production, it was often brewed at home, but there were also commercial stone beer breweries operating in Carinthia. Carinthian stone beer can also be considered to have been an farmhouse ale: when the Austrian government, in the middle of the eighteenth century, tried to supplant this beer style with more modern beers, Primus Felician Kerkho, the lawyer of the Viktring abbey who had been asked for his expert opinion, wrote that stone beer (besides water) was the only drink available to field workers on farms, and taking stone beer away from farmers would only deny them their refreshments after a week of hard work. Another aspect was that farmers used oats and low-quality wheat for brewing instead of the more highly valued barley and wheat. They malted these low-quality grains themselves using simple smoke kilns fired with cherry wood[67, p.154]. After brewing, the spent grains could be then even be used for feeding the livestock, which in turn produced fertiliser. If farmers would have to get used to more modern beer, it would be not only an additional burden on them because they'd have to get metal tuns, but also the local grain production would have had to change in the Viktring district since not enough barley was grown to supplant the oats used in brewing[17].

In the second half of the 19th century, stone beer declined massively in Carinthia. From about 60 breweries, only two of them remained in the beginning of the 20th century, in particular the Holzleger brewery by Valentin Kaschitz and the brewery J. Ure in Waidmannsdorf (nowadays part of the city of Klagenfurt)[17].

Not much is known about the stone beer brewing methods in Styria. What is known though is that stone beer brewing existed alongside "kettle brewing" at least since the 16th century. Over time, the kettle brewing method gradually took over, especially since brewing guilds were formed and these guilds launched legal battles against stone brewing: in 1721, all authorities were obliged to enforce that brewing in brew houses could only be done by trained brewers. Untrained owners of brew houses had to hire them, otherwise they were threatened with the confiscation of their brewing equipment, malt, and beer. Also, all millers, innkeepers and farmers were prohibited from brewing for sale, under threat of confiscation of their equipment[47, p.166]. In some of these legal battles, stone beer brewers were still successful in claiming a customary right of brewing.

In 1773, a beer taxation law was enacted in Styria which both allowed stone and kettle brewing. Stone beer was taxed with 9 Kreuzer per Eimer, while kettle beer was taxed with 18 Kreuzer per Eimer. The same ratio of 1:2 was also in place for the retail price. But stone brewers were still at a disadvantage as they were not allowed to use anything but hot stones for heating, and only allowed to use oats as grain for brewing[47, p.170]. Any stone brewer who was caught brewing with other ingredients such as barley or wheat, or using kettles or coppers, or employing trained brewers, would have their equipment confiscated and lose their brewing rights for life. The same law also explicitly prohibited homebrewing for own consumption for everyone who hadn't previously owned brewing rights[47, pp.170-171].

This law led to stone brewers complaining that they had always brewed using both barley and oats, and they could prove it using old documents since the beer taxation law specifically referred to old customary brewing rights. This in turn led to complaints by kettle brewers that the stone beer was "too good and almost brewed like in the style of kettle beer", which made it hard to compete with since the stone beer was only half the price[47, p.171].

Outside of Carinthia and Styria, stone beer brewing traditions existed in large parts of Northern Europe, in particular Norway, Finland, Estonia, and Denmark[20]. Modern German stone beer is quite different from this type of stone beer: it usually involves dropping super-heated stones into the boiling wort to caramelise some of the sugars in the wort. Other than the name, this beer has very little to do with the traditional beer style of stone beers.

The recipe presented here is a version more reminiscent of 19th century stone beer: oat malt was only used in small amounts, while the grist mostly consisted of barley malt and some wheat malt. The original gravity of 9 °P (1.036) is on the upper end of the scale, while less strong versions of this beer were often brewed at a strength of 6 to 7 °P (1.024 to 1.028)[17].

Recipe

- OG 9 °P (1.036)
- 4% ABV
- 10 IBU

Ingredients

- 2 kg (4.17 lb) Vienna malt (60.6%)
- 0.8 kg (1.67 lb) pale wheat malt (24.2%)

- 0.5 kg (1.04 lb) oat malt (15.2%)
- 50 g (1.67 oz) leaf hops (3% alpha acid)
- 1 pack top-fermenting yeast, e.g. WLP029
- 30 fist-sized graywacke or granite stones (e.g. cobblestones)
- juniper branches

Mashing

- The stones need to be heated beforehand on a barbecue grill, ideally until they glow red
- Put juniper branches on the bottom of the mash/lauter tun, they will act as mash filter
- Add 2 litres (0.5 gal) of cold liquor to the mash tun
- Add some of the hot stones until the water begins to boil
- Add hops and boil for 10 minutes
- Add 7 litres (1.75 gal) of cold liquor
- Dough in Vienna malt and oat malt
- Slowly add hot stones while continuously stirring the mash until the mash begins to boil
- After 10 minutes of boiling, add 5 litres (1.25 gal) of cold liquor
- Dough in wheat malt, the mash should now have a temperature of about 65 to 68 °C (149 to 154.4 °F)
- Rest for 1 hour
- Lauter and sparge with 70 °C (158 °F) hot liquor directly into the fermenter until about 20 litres (5 gal) of wort have been collected

Fermentation

- Chill wort to about 20 °C (68 °F)
- Pitch yeast

Alternative Grist   Instead of the provided grist, you can also use an alternative grist of 50% barley malt and 50% oat malt or even 100% oat malt, optionally with a small amount of wheat malt. Make sure to keep a small amount of malt for the second dough-in after the mash boil. Also take into account that oat malt provides a lower extract than barley malt or wheat malt. The remaining brewing process can be conducted as described above.

You can also reduce the grist to reach an original gravity of only 6 or 7 °P (1.024 to 1.028) to match the more common strength of this beer.

9.3 Vienna Lager

During his time of training at the Simmering brewery in Vienna, Anton Dreher, the son of the then-owner of the Kleinschwechater brewery in Kleinschwechat near Vienna, met Gabriel Sedlmayr, the son of the then-owner of the Spaten brewery in Munich, and befriended him. They shared a common ethos and a view of how to conduct business, and therefore decided to travel through Germany and England to learn more about brewing. In 1832, he left Vienna to meet Sedlmayr in Munich, from where they travelled onwards via Frankfurt and Hamburg to London. The purpose of their journey to Great Britain was to research and document local brewing technologies.

When they'd arrived in London, they quickly learned that English breweries were not open to visiting foreigners, unlike Munich, where Bavarian sociability made breweries open their doors even for strangers. Dreher therefore decided to start working in a large London brewery to be able to take a closer look at the operations, but only for as long as necessary to get an overview over the inside of the brewery itself. In Burton upon Trent, Dreher and Sedlmayr were lucky to learn to know Sir Bass, who would invite them for a fox hunt, and allow them entrance to his brewery. With a letter of recommendation from him, they moved on to visit other breweries in Glasgow and Edinburgh. This gave them the opporunity to learn more about the specifically British brewing methods which they wanted to use at home. British malting was one main area that turned out to be superior to German and Austrian techniques, while lots of other methods were not applicable in German lager brewing.

Dreher and Sedlmayr returned to Munich, where they stayed over the winter 1832/33 and spent time conducting brewing experiments and trying out their newly gained knowledge[24].

After returning to Vienna, Anton Dreher took over the Kleinschwechater brewery from his mother in April 1836, was able to modernise it after he fully gained ownership in 1838, and began to produce pale malt to brew Munich-style lager beer. The pale malt gave an amber-coloured wort which was clearly lighter than brown malts at that time, but still darker than Pilsner malt nowadays, and was henceforth known as Vienna malt.

An original recipe for Vienna lager is not directly documented. The recipe in this book is reconstructed based on recordings of the original and final gravity of Vienna lager from 1870[44, p.58]. Since Vienna malt was especially made to produce Vienna lager, it can be assumed that it was used exclusively to brew this beer.

Since the early 1860's, the Kleinschwechater brewery owned land in Michelob/Měcholupy in Bohemia[24, pp.24-25] to grow hops and brewing barley to be completely self-sufficient and independent from the volatile hop and barley markets[3, p.391]. Michelob/Měcholupy is just 7 kilometres south of Saaz/Žatec, so it can also be assumed that most likely Saazer hops or a very similar land race were grown there, and eventually used by the brewery for Vienna lager. From other historic sources we also know that the beer was hopped at 4 grams per litre[49, p.369].

In a *Festschrift* from 1941 about the 100 year anniversary of production of *Schwechater Lager*, a water colour painting of the hop storage also shows hop bales with the letters "SAAZ" on them. This is an additional indicator that at least for some time, Kleinschwechater brewery used Saazer hops.

Anton Dreher died unexpectedly in 1863. By 1871, Dreher's son and heir, Anton Dreher the younger, owned four breweries in total: Kleinschwechat near Vienna, Steinbruch/Kőbánya near Pest (which is now Budapest), Michelob/Měcholupy in Bohemia, and Trieste[13, p.11], which produced in total more than 1 million Eimer (about 565000 hl) of beer, amounting to about 5% of the total beer production in the Austrian-Hungarian Empire.

Recipe (1870)

- OG 13 °P (1.053)
- 4.6% ABV
- 30 IBU
- 8.6 EBC (4.3 SRM)

Ingredients

- 4.2 kg (8.77 lb) Vienna malt (100%)
- 80 g (2.67 oz) Saazer hops (3% alpha acid)
- 1 pack bottom-fermenting yeast, e.g. WLP820 or WLP920

Mashing

- Mash, lauter and sparge like Munich Lagerbier
- Collect only 26 litres (6.5 gal) of wort

Wort Boil

- Boil wort for 90 minutes

Fermentation

- Ferment the same as Munich Lagerbier, but reduce the lagering time to 40 to 60 days

9.4 Prague Beer

Bohemia has had a strong brewing tradition for centuries. Prague was one of the centres of beer brewing, and its beers were prized not only in Bohemia and Austria, but even in Germany. Most likely due to geographical proximity, brewing in Prague was very much like in Bavarian brewing, but it is reported that even though there was lager brewing in Bohemia, beer in Prague was brewed in a top-fermented fashion at least as late as the 1830's. Despite that, the beer was still matured in ice cellars for at least 4 to 6 weeks, and was served ice-cold to customers[5, pp.31-33].

Recipe (1834)

- OG 16.5 °P (1.068)
- 6.6% ABV
- 86 IBU
- 11.8 EBC (6 SRM)

Ingredients

- 5.7 kg (11.9 lb) Vienna malt (100%)
- 300 g (10 oz) Saazer hops (3% alpha acid)
- 1 pack top-fermenting yeast, e.g. WLP029

Mashing

- Dough in with 20 litres (5 gal) of liquor at 50 °C (122 °F), 1 hour rest

- Add 8 litres (2 gal) of boiling liquor until temperature has reached 63 °C (145.4 °F)

- Draw 4.5 litres (1.12 gal) of thick mash, bring to a boil, mix back until mash has reached 68 °C (154.4 °F), then 1 hour rest

- Draw 16 litres (4 gal) of thin mash, bring to a boil, mix back until mash has reached 84 °C (183.2 °F)

- Lauter, sparge with 78 °C (172.4 °F) hot liquor until about 26 litres (6.5 gal) of wort have been collected

Wort Boil

- Boil wort for 90 minutes

- Add hops 45 minutes before the end of the boil

Fermentation

- Chill wort to 20 °C (68 °F)

- Pitch yeast

- After the end of the fermentation, chill beer down to 2 to 4 °C (35.6 to 39.2 °F), mature for 4 to 6 weeks.

Chapter 10

Converting Historic Recipes

In order to convert historic recipes into a form that is usable for homebrewers, some knowledge is necessary how brewing instructions were structured in the 18th and 19th century.

First of all, there's the problem of units. Before the efforts to standardise and systematise them in the 19th century, for example through the introduction of the metric system or the Imperial unit system, there was an absolute chaos of different units for dry volume, liquid volume and weights. In particular thanks to German *Kleinstaaterei*, there existed a large amount of local units that often bore the same name, but were more or less different to each other. Also, certain units were redefined multiple times, so in order to exactly interpret quantities, it is necessary to know where an author was from or which audience a text would be targeting, and additionally, when it was written.

Besides the problem of units also exists the problem of types of units. This specifically shows in how the amount of malt was specified in recipes. While nowadays a grist would be described by weight or percentage of the different ingredients, back in the day just providing amounts of malt as dry volume was more common. After all, it is more practical to measure bulk goods such as malt in pails instead of weighing them. In order to be able to derive the weight from a certain volume of malt, it is necessary to know the density of the malt. With barley malt, you can assume a density of about 350 to 450 kg per cubic meter.

And third, there's the language. If you don't know the language in which the recipes were written, it is hard to interpret them. In particular with German, since it was printed in its very own Gothic font until the end of the 19th century, which makes it even harder to read: the long 's' is hard to distinguish from 'f', 't' can sometimes look similar to 'k', which in turn can be very similar to 'x', especially when the lead letters are a bit worn, the 'sz' ligature can look to the 'tz' ligature, and so on. But even for native speakers, outdated idioms, sentence structures and vocabulary that slightly shifted meaning in the last 150 to 200 years can complicate things.

10.1 Units

Dry Volume: Scheffel, Metze

The Berliner Scheffel, also known as Prussian Scheffel, is equivalent to 54.91 litres. Before 1818, the "old" Scheffel was also valid, which was equivalent to 54.728 litres. Therefore, for a Scheffel of barley malt you can assume a weight of 19.2 to 24.7 kg.

In Bavaria on the other hand there existed the Bavarian Scheffel, which was equivalent to 222.357 litres. In addition to that, there also existed the Munich grain Scheffel with 222.2 litres, and the oat Scheffel with 343 litres. In total, there existed over a hundred different definitions of a unit named Scheffel all over Germany.

The Metze is another unit for dry volume. As with the Scheffel, its actual size great differs depending on which local definition from which time period is used. In Prussia, a Metze was about 3.42 litres until 1816, and 3.435 litres from 1816 on. In Bavaria, the Metze was defined as 34 2/3, or 1/6 Scheffel, and therefore equivalent to 37.0596 litres. In Austria, a Metze was 61.487 litres, while in Nuremberg different Metzen for grain (20.5 litres) and oats (19.2 litres) were in use.

Liquid Volume: Quart, Tonne, Eimer

To measure liquid volume, two very common units in Prussia were the Quart of 1.145 litres, and the Tonne, which was equivalent to 100 Quart. In Bavaria, the Maß of 1.069 litres was rather common. Another widely used unit was the Eimer (literally "bucket"): in Bavaria, there were at least two different ones, the Schenkeimer (64.14 litres), and the Biereimer (68.52 litres). In historic literature the distinction is often not made, so readers have to interpret by themselves which one to use. In Austria, the Eimer was equivalent to 56.589 litres.

Weight: Pfund and Loth

The Pfund was used for weights (see the English cognate "pound"). It also had different meanings: in Prussia, until 1816, the old Cölln Mark weight system was still valid. In that system, a Pfund was 467.622 g. Starting 1816, the new Prussian weight system was enacted, where a Pfund was equivalent to 468.53588 g. In Bavaria, the Viennese Pfund was the standard unit, which since the middle ages was equivalent to 561.288 g. In 1811, the Bavarian system was simplified, and the Bavarian Pfund was standardised as exactly 560 g. For smaller amounts, the Loth was common, which was 17.54025 g before 1811 and 17.5 g after 1811 in Bavaria. In

Prussia, the Loth was defined as 14.613 g respectively 14.642 g since 1816.

Temperature: Réaumur and Fahrenheit

Temperatures were also specified differently. While in English-speaking literature Fahrenheit was the most common unit, German-speaking literature often preferred the Réaumur scale. With Réaumur, the freezing temperature of water is at 0 °Re, while the boiling temperature is at 80 °Re. This similarity to the Celsius scale makes it tricky, since temperature specifications can very easily get misinterpreted as Celsius even though they're actually meant as Réaumur. In areas like mashing, where keeping exact temperatures is absolutely crucial, a deviation by a factor of 1.25 would be highly problematic and yield entirely different results.

10.2 Converting a Recipe by Example

Converting an old recipe can be done in two big steps: first, the units of all ingredients need to be determined and converted to modern units. When this conversion is done, the recipe can then be scaled down to a size that is suitable for homebrewers using the rule of three.

I'd like to present this using a practical example: in order to produce 2000 Quart of beer, a recipe prescribes using 12 Berliner Scheffel of pale barley malt (most likely similar to Pilsner malt), 10 Scheffel of pale wheat malt, and 3 Pfund of hops.

First we'll convert the amounts of ingredients and beer to modern units. One Quart is equivalent to 1.145 litres, 2000 Quart of beer are therefore 2000 * 1.145 = 2290 litres.

For a Berliner Scheffel, we can assume a weight of about 24 kg. 12 Scheffel of barley malt are therefore 12 * 24 = 288 kg, while 10 Scheffel of wheat malt are 10 * 24 = 240 kg.

The Berliner Pfund is equivalent to 468.5 g. 3 Pfund of hops are therefore 3 * 468.5 = 1405.5 g hops. A German land race with a low amount of alpha acid seems suitable here. The ingredients we have so far are these:

- 288 kg Pilsner malt

- 240 kg pale wheat malt

- 1405.5 g hops

These ingredients are for 2290 litres of beer, though. Since homebrewers only want to brew smaller amounts like 20 litres of beer at once, we need to scale the amount of ingredients: 2290 / 20 = 114.5. We will correct the amounts by this factor:

- 288 / 114.5 = 2.515 kg Pilsner malt

- 240 / 114.5 = 2.096 kg pale wheat malt

- 1405.5 / 114.5 = 12.275 g hops

For practical reasons, these amounts can be rounded to 2.5 kg, 2.1 kg, and 12 g.

Chapter 11

Acknowledgments and Dedications

First and foremost, I would like to thank my wife Louise for enduring me and my cranky side as well as listening to many of my random beer-related facts I bombarded her with while I was conducting research for this book. Without her patience and encouragement, I would have never been able to finish this book, so I dedicate this book to her.

I would also like to thank Rory Lawton, who guided and taught the Berlin craft beer scene that has formed and grown immensely in the last five years, and regularly brought together enthusiastic Berlin homebrewers from all walks of life. His efforts in building these communities greatly influenced my interest in beer and its history.

For reviewing the book and giving me honest and helpful feedback and advice, I would also like to thank (in no particular order) Joe Stange, Ron Pattinson, Stan Hieronymus and Benedikt Rausch.

Chapter 12

Glossary

alpha acid: a class of chemical compounds found in hops. When isomerised, e.g. through boiling, they provide bitterness in beer.

amylase: a number of enzymes that convert complex starches into simpler fermentable and non-fermentable sugars.

attenuation: the percentage of sugar that is converted to alcohol and carbon dioxide by the yeast during fermentation.

bottom-fermenting yeast: yeast of the species *Saccharomyces pastorianus* that ferments at low temperatures of typically 8 to 12 °C and is used to produce lager beers. Historically, this type of yeast was harvested from the bottom of the fermenter.

Brettanomyces: a type of yeast with a slower metabolism than brewers yeast and the ability to ferment more complex carbohydrates. Due to its production of off-flavours, it is classed as a spoiling agent in most beers, but is important in the production of British stock ales, Berliner Weisse and spontaneously fermented Belgian beers.

diastatic power: the ability of malt to convert complex carbohydrates (starch) to simple sugars through amylase enzymes. The larger the amount of starch a certain amount of malt can convert to simple sugars, the higher the diastatic power.

final gravity: the remaining amount of fermentable and non-fermentable sugars in a beer after fermentation.

fining: substances that are added to wort or beer in order to produce clear beer by removing haze.

green malt: grain that has germinated but has not yet been dried.

grist: the composition of malts and their respective amounts that are used to produce wort.

kiln: a device to dry green malt using a heat source, such as hot air or smoke.

landrace: a cultivated, locally adapted, traditional variety of a plant such as hops.

lautering: the process of separating the liquid portion from the hard matter of the mash.

liquor: brewing jargon for water that is used for brewing. Liquor is used for brewing, water is used for cleaning.

malt: grain that has germinated through the application of water and then was dried after the grain was modified enough by the germination process in order to be useful for brewing.

mash: a mix of ground up malt with liquor that is kept at temperatures that allow the amylase enzymes to convert the malt's starch to sugar.

modification: the amount of which the internal structure of a grain has been changed through germination.

original gravity: the amount of fermentable and non-fermentable sugars in a wort before fermentation starts.

sparge: the process of sprinkling water on top of a mash in order to rinse out sugars during lautering.

top-fermenting yeast: yeast of the species *Saccharomyces cerevisiae* that usually ferments at around room temperature. Historically, this type of yeast was harvested from the top of the fermenter.

wort: a liquid that is extracted from a mash by lautering. It contains sugars that have been converted from the starches in the malt through its enzymes.

yeast: single-celled fungi. In the context of brewing, this usually describes yeast varieties that are used for fermentation, such as Saccharomyces and Brettanomyces.

Chapter 13

Bibliography

[1] In: *Regensburger Zeitung, 20. April 1841* (1841). URL: https://books.google.de/books?id=By5EAAAAcAAJ%5C&pg=PP467.

[2] In: (). URL: http://www.pspd.org.pl/uploads/grodziskie/graetzer-brauwelt-1990.pdf.

[3] *Allgemeine Deutsche Biographie. Band 5*. Leipzig, 1877. URL: https://de.wikisource.org/w/index.php?title=ADB:Dreher,_Anton&oldid=616231.

[4] Agnes Bartscherer. "Die Leipziger Studenten Johann Wolfgang Goethe und Horn und die Biere in Leipzig und Umland". In: *Gesellschaft für die Geschichte und Bibliographie des Brauwesens E.V. Jahrbuch 1954* (1954), pp. 57–94.

[5] David Booth. *The Art of Brewing*. London, 1834. URL: https://play.google.com/books/reader?id=9xgZAAAAYAAJ.

[6] Anton Bosch. *Biographie von Anton Bosch*. Vienna, 1868. URL: https://books.google.de/books?id=vxG0ixeF8pQC.

[7] Dr. Richard Braungart. *Der Hopfen aller hopfenbauenden Länder der Erde als Braumaterial*. Munich & Leipzig, 1901. URL: https://archive.org/details/derhopfenallerho00brauuoft.

[8] Franc. Ern. Brückmann. *Epistola Itineraria XXXVIII. De Cerevisia Goslariensi*. Wolfenbüttel, 1735. URL: http://herrrausch.de/gose/CervesiaGoslarensisBesser.pdf.

[9] Rudolf M. Buchner. *Vergangenheit und Gegenwart Steirischer Bierbrauereien*. 1993.

[10] *Codex Austriacus*. Vienna, 1704. URL: https://books.google.de/books?id=i1hSDgXpN7OC.

[11] G. F. Eduard Crusius. *Geschichte der vormals Kaiserlichen freien Reichsstadt Goslar am Harze*. Osterode, 1842. URL: https://play.google.com/books/reader?id=qGQAAAAAcAAJ.

[12] *Der schwäbische Bierbrauer*. Waldsee, 1874. URL: https://play.google.com/books/reader?id=Ad5kAAAAcAAJ.

[13] *Die Bierproduktion in Oesterreich-Ungarn, im Deutschen Reich, in Grossbritannien und Irland, Belgien, Frankreich, den Niederlanden, Schweden und Norwegen, Russland und Nord-Amerika*. Vienna, 1873. URL: http://reader.digitale-sammlungen.de/de/fs1/object/display/bsb11162159_00005.html.

[14] *Die Geschichte des fränkischen Hopfenbaues nebst einer Betrachtung der Entwicklung und Organisation des Nürnberger Hopfenmarktes*. Nuremberg, 1915. URL: https://goo.gl/5LTtFA.

[15] Dr. Franz Döbereiner. *Beschreibung der Fabrikation des Braunbiers in Bayern*. Jena, 1849. URL: http://digital.slub-dresden.de/werkansicht/dlf/1979/1/.

[16] A. Dörfel. *Die Herstellung obergäriger Biere und die Malzbierbrauerei Groterjan A.G. in Berlin*. Berlin, 1947. URL: https://s3-eu-west-1.amazonaws.com/andreasdotorg-bucket/Groterjan-Doerfel.pdf.

[17] Raimund Dürnwirth. *Vom Steinbier*. Klagenfurt, 1905. URL: https://de.wikisource.org/wiki/Vom_Steinbier.

[18] *Fest-Schrift herausgegeben zur Erinnerung an die 30jährige Lehrthätigkeit im Braufache des Herrn Karl Michel*. 1899.

[19] "Fragen und Antworten zum Reinheitsgebot". In: (). URL: https://goo.gl/jvv5iW.

[20] Lars Marius Garshol. "How stone beer was brewed". In: (2016). URL: http://www.garshol.priv.no/blog/361.html.

[21] Hans-Erdmann Gringer. "Auch Goethe kam auf den Geschmack". In: (2009). URL: http://www.mz-web.de/merseburg/auch-goethe-kam-auf-den-geschmack-8122890.

[22] Dr. Julius Ludwig Gumbinner. *Handbuch der praktischen Bierbrauerei*. Berlin, 1845. URL: https://play.google.com/books/reader?id=9S5FAAAAYAAJ.

[23] Philipp Heiß. *Die Bierbrauerei mit besonderer Berücksichtigung der Dickmaischbrauerei*. Munich, 1853.

[24] Eduard Hensel. *Anton Dreher. Biographische Skizze*. Vienna, 1864. URL: https://play.google.com/books/reader?id=v2McUMoZX9OC.

[25] Sigism. Friedr. Hermbstädt. *Chemische Grundsätze der Kunst Bier zu brauen*. Berlin, 1826. URL: https://play.google.com/books/reader?id=ESpeAAAAcAAJ.

[26] A. Herrmann. *Der bayerische Bierbrauer in der Malztenne, im Brauhause und Gährkeller, dann beim Gersten- und Hopfen-Einkaufe etc.* Nürnberg, 1839. URL: https://opacplus.bsb-muenchen.de/Vta2/bsb10374470/bsb:BV001677739.

[27] Fr. Hofmann. "Ein Geheimniß im Bierreiche." In: (1872). URL: https://de.wikisource.org/wiki/Ein_Geheimni%C3%9F_im_Bierreiche.

[28] Johann Christoph Jordan. *Anweisung zum kunstmäßigen Brauen des Weißbiers*. Hannover, 1799. URL: http://gdz.sub.uni-goettingen.de/dms/load/toc/?PID=PPN672719770.

[29] *Katechismus des Braumeisters oder leichtfaßliche Anleitung, die Meisterprüfung der Bierbrauerei nach den Anforderungen der neuesten gesetzlichen Bestimmungen bestehen zu können*. München, 1865. URL: https://play.google.com/books/reader?id=efs6AAAAcAAJ.

[30] David Kellner. *Hochnutzbar und bewährte edle Bierbrau-Kunst.* Leipzig & Gotha, 1690. URL: http://digital.slub-dresden.de/werkansicht/dlf/9131/1/.

[31] Andreas Krennmair. "Horner Bier". In: (2016). URL: http://dafteejit.com/2016/01/horner-bier/.

[32] A. Kulitzscher. *Handbuch zur Fabrikation obergäriger Biere.* Berlin, 1930.

[33] Johann C. Leuchs. *Vollständige Braukunde, oder wissenschaftlich-praktische Darstellung der Bierbrauerei in ihrem ganzen Umfange und nach den neuesten Verbesserungen.* Nürnberg, 1831. URL: https://play.google.com/books/reader?id=eDA7AAAAcAAJ.

[34] Gerolf Annemüller / Hans-J. Manger / Peter Lietz. *Die Berliner Weiße - Ein Stück Berliner Geschichte.* Berlin, 2008.

[35] Johann Adam Messerschmitt. *Die Bamberger Bierbrauerei.* Bamberg, 1836. URL: https://play.google.com/books/reader?id=3TI7AAAAcAAJ.

[36] Friedrich Meyer. *Die bayerische Bierbrauerei in allen ihren Theilen und wie solche in den vorzüglichsten Bierbrauereien im Königreiche Bayern dermalen betrieben wird; dann die Branntweinbrennerei u. Essigfabrikation, soweit solche mit der Bierbrauerei verbunden scheinen, so wie das Nöthige über den Hopfen und den Hopfenbau.* Nürnberg, 1847. URL: http://www.bsb-muenchen-digital.de/~web/web1037/bsb10376454/images/index.html.

[37] Friedrich Meyer. *Die bayerische Bierbrauerei oder die Brauerei der braunen Biere und des weißen Gerstenbieres, wie solche in den vorzüglichsten Brauereien in Bayern dermalen betrieben wird, dann die mit der Bierbrauerei verbundene Branntweinbrennerei, Fruchtessigsiederei und das einem Brauer Nöthige über den Hopfen und den Hopfenbau.* Ansbach, 1830. URL: http://reader.digitale-sammlungen.de/de/fs1/object/display/bsb10388118_00005.html.

[38] Carl Michel. *Geschichte des Bieres von der ältesten Zeit bis zum Jahre 1899.* Augsburg, 1899. URL: http://daten.digitale-sammlungen.de/~db/0007/bsb00074275/images/.

[39] P. Müller. *Handbuch für Bierbrauer.* Braunschweig, 1854. URL: https://play.google.com/books/reader?id=UTw7AAAAcAAJ.

[40] *München und die Münchener.* Karlsruhe (Baden), 1905. URL: https://archive.org/stream/bub_gb_zptKAAAAMAAJ.

[41] Johann Philipp Christian Muntz. *Das Bierbrauen in allen seinen Zweigen, als Mälzen, Gähren, Schroten, Hopfen, etc. mit Bemerkungen und Verfahrungsarten bei dem Brauen in Baiern, am Rheine, in Franken etc.* Plauen, 1840. URL: http://digital.slub-dresden.de/werkansicht/dlf/2290/4/.

[42] Leo Nast. *Die Berliner Brauindustrie.* Berlin, 1916. URL: https://archive.org/stream/dieberlinerbraui00nast.

[43] Patie. *Kurzer Abriß des Fabriken-, Gewerbe-, und HandlungsZustandes in den ChurBraunschweig-Lüneburgischen Landen.* Göttingen, 1796. URL: https://books.google.de/books?id=eBRRAAAAcAAJ.

[44] Ronald Pattinson. "Decoction!" In: (2011).

[45] Franz Andreas Paupie. *Die Kunst des Bierbrauens, physisch-chemisch-ökonomisch beschrieben, erster Theil.* Prague, 1820. URL: https://archive.org/stream/bub_gb_lidSAAAAcAAJ.

[46] Hermann Pfauth. *Neuestes illustriertes Taschenbuch der Bayerischen Bierbrauerei mit Berücksichtigung der wichtigsten theoretischen Sätze.* Stuttgart, 1870. URL: https://opacplus.bsb-muenchen.de/Vta2/bsb10704296/bsb:BV014205730.

[47] Franz Pichler. "Das Steinbierbrauen in der Steiermark". In: *Zeitschrift des Historischen Vereines für Steiermark* (1962), pp. 155–173.

[48] Johann Heinrich Moritz Poppe. *Die Bierbrauerey auf der höchsten Stufe der jetzigen Vollkommenheit.* Tübingen, 1826. URL: https://play.google.com/books/reader?id=fsVaAAAAcAAJ.

[49] Dr. W. Prausnitz. *Grundzüge der Hygiene*. Munich & Leipzig, 1892. URL: https://archive.org/details/b24996300.

[50] Benedikt Rausch. In: (2017). URL: http://wilder-wald.com/2017/02/15/gosslarsche-gose/.

[51] Benedikt Rausch. In: (2017). URL: http://wilder-wald.com/2017/07/26/gose-yeast/.

[52] Wilhelm Herrmann Georg Remer. *Lehrbuch der polizeilich-gerichtlichen Chemie*. Helmstädt, 1812. URL: https://archive.org/details/lehrbuchderpoliz00reme.

[53] "report on the state of works of the PSPD (Polish Homebrewers Association) commission for the Grodziskie beer". In: (2012). URL: http://www.pspd.org.pl/uploads/grodziskie/grodziskie-redivivus-raport-1-eng.pdf.

[54] Klaus Rupprecht. "Reinheitsgebot, 1516". In: (2016). URL: https://www.historisches-lexikon-bayerns.de/Lexikon/Reinheitsgebot,_1516.

[55] Josef Benno Sailer. *Münchener Bier-Chronik*. 1929. URL: http://daten.digitale-sammlungen.de/~db/0004/bsb00049116/images/.

[56] Josef Benno Sailer. *Münchner Oktoberfest*. Munich, 1932. URL: http://daten.digitale-sammlungen.de/~db/0004/bsb00048887/images/index.html.

[57] *Sammlung von Natur- und Medicin- Wie auch hierzu gehörigen Kunst- und Literatur-Geschichten*. Breslau, 1726. URL: https://books.google.de/books?id=Q_BWAAAAcAAJ.

[58] Benno Scharl. *Beschreibung der Braunbier-Brauerey im Königreiche Baiern*. München, 1814.

[59] Adolf Schmidl. *Wien's Umgebungen auf zwanzig Stunden im Umkreise*. Vienna, 1835. URL: https://books.google.de/books?id=MTxiAAAAcAAJ.

[60] Carl Wilhelm Schmidt. *Die Bierbrauerei in ihrem ganzen Umfange*. Züllichau, 1820. URL: http://digital.slub-dresden.de/werkansicht/dlf/2291/1/.

[61] Gustav Schmoller. *Staats- und socialwissenschaftliche Forschungen*. Leipzig, 1898. URL: https://archive.org/stream/staatsundsozial15unkngoog.

[62] "Schneider Weisse auf dem Oktoberfest". In: (). URL: https://www.bayerische-landesbibliothek-online.de/oktoberfest-schneider.

[63] Dr. Franz Schönfeld. *Die Herstellung obergähriger Biere*. Berlin, 1902.

[64] Dr. Franz Schönfeld. *Obergärige Biere und ihre Herstellung*. Berlin, 1939.

[65] J.S. Schorer. *Ausführliches Lehrbuch der Bayrischen Bierbrauerei mit besonderer Berücksichtigung der Dickmaischbrauerei*. Altona, 1863.

[66] Johann Albert Joseph Seifert. *Das Bamberger Bier*. Bamberg, 1818.

[67] Wolfgang Dieter Speckmann. *Biere die Geschichte machten*. 2005. ISBN: 3870233133.

[68] *Vermischte oeconomische Sammlungen*. Leipzig, 1750. URL: https://play.google.com/books/reader?id=A1c7AAAAcAAJ.

[69] "Wall chart in the German Museum Munich". In: (). URL: http://hobbybrauer.de/modules.php?name=eBoard%5C&file=viewthread%5C&tid=7753.

[70] Johann Wilhelm Wäser. *Gründliche Anleitung zum Bierbrauen, zur Beförderung richtiger Grundsätze der vorzüglichen Bereitung das Braun- Weiß- und Englisch-Bier betreffend in systematischer Ordnung und in Berechnungen tabellarisch dargestellt*. Berlin, 1793. URL: https://play.google.com/books/reader?id=aG87AAAAcAAJ.

Made in the USA
Middletown, DE
29 May 2021